SPOTLIGHT OF LOVE

INSIGHTS AND SKILLS
FOR COUPLES

CHELI LANGE, LPC

NEW DEGREE PRESS

Illustrations by Michael Scott
Cover design by Donna Cunningham

SPOTLIGHT OF LOVE
Insights and Skills for Couples

ISBN   979-8-88504-545-2 *Paperback*
            979-8-88504-871-2 *Kindle Ebook*
            979-8-88504-661-9 *Ebook*

SPOTLIGHT OF LOVE

For Tyler, Cameron, and Grant,
who inspired me to start writing,
and for Jim and Joanna,
who wouldn't let me stop.

CONTENTS

AUTHOR'S NOTE

While the *Spotlight of Love*, just like love itself, is limitless, my articulation of it most certainly is not. I work to reduce my biases while recognizing I can only ever see through my own lens. I value reader feedback and trust that ongoing conversations about what deeply matters will expand our capacities for loving relationships. I will learn something tomorrow I don't know today, and for that I am grateful—even though sometimes the lessons hurt like hell.

As you read the following chapters in which I suggest some radical phrases for partners to use, you might think, *Cheli, people just don't talk like this!* Yes, I get it! I've learned these particular phrases as sentence starters because they are concise and a little different, and therefore most people remember them easily. If you have other words that you and your partner experience as inviting and validating, and you can recall them in stressful moments, that's great. The aim is clarity and reconnection, and there are many paths.

This book offers strategies for you to try on and see how they fit for you. Deciding whether or not to use them and understanding *why* is a valuable process. Sometimes the strategies weave together. Sometimes they stand alone. Most are based on research by leading professionals in the fields of trauma and couples therapies. All reflect my experience as a therapist and my time as a person learning about love and interconnection. This book is in no way intended as a substitute for therapy. Rather, these pages contain insights about therapy and skills for partners to use with each other. I will share examples from many types of relationships in addition to those of romantic partners because sometimes a skill is easier to absorb when imagined in a different context.

If you suspect you might be in an abusive relationship, I recommend finding a licensed professional who is trained and experienced in this area before engaging in couples therapy or asking your partner to join you for any of the Spotlight Moves or exercises in this book. Additional thoughts on trauma and what to look for in a therapist can be found at the end of Chapter 4.

Any names or direct quotes in the book are shared with the permission of generous nonclient interviewees. The partner dialogue comes from frequently heard phrases that represent no particular gender, couple, or person, even though the voices of my clients live in me as reminders of their courage, resilience, and all the good that can happen when you keep showing up.

Thank you, dear reader, for showing up! All proceeds of this book are donated to the Trauma Recovery, EMDR Humanitarian Assistance Programs, which provide trauma-informed therapy to survivors and first responders in the wake of natural or man-made disasters throughout the world.

INTRODUCTION

———

A couple enters my office. Walking past the red wingback chairs, they opt for the love seat.

"We keep having the same fight over and over." Sideways glance, though their eyes don't meet.

"What was it about this time?"

"I can't even remember..." They both pause, turning to each other, searching their shared memory for what started it all. "Oh, the dishes."

"Right, the dishes. I put them the wrong way." Nearly identical sighs of exasperation.

They look back to me. "There's so much that's good between us... and then... something happens, and it's like we're suddenly on opposite sides."

*   *   *

"Opposite sides." What a frustrating and confusing experience for this couple. They love each other. "There's so much that's good," they say, and it's true: Partners can get disconnected pretty quickly. Versions of this story are common for couples at any stage of the relationship. Even when a big event has caused the disconnection (e.g., an affair, a job loss, a death in the family, etc.), a difficult repeating pattern of interaction often lurks underneath, keeping them from being a reliable source of comfort for each other when that's what they need most.

In this book, we will explore various topics including how to give to each other more generously and receive more courageously; what a drama triangle is and how to exit that thing as quickly as possible; how to regulate the metaphorical heat on the burners of your very real relationship; and ways to think about the goodness of fit between you at different stages.

In his book *How to Love*, Tibetan monk and teacher Thich Nhat Hanh highlights the essential nature of secure relationships. In terms of the Vietnamese language, this nature is embedded in the very naming of life partners, who refer to each other simply as what translates as *my home*. Imagine establishing or reestablishing a relational foundation so strong and flexible that *home* can be found in the shape, the manner, the very expression of the one you love, wherever you are.

Dr. Sue Johnson, clinical psychologist and developer of Emotionally Focused Therapy (EFT) for couples, describes the core nature of love as "our bulwark, designed to provide emotional protection so we can cope with the ups and downs of existence… We need emotional attachments with a few irreplaceable others to be physically and mentally healthy—to survive."

Healthy partnerships not only bring happiness to us but also to our children and their children. By loving well and demonstrating a balanced flow of giving and receiving, we offer a positive model for how relationships can be. This contribution to the life of families is my primary motivation for writing.

What Stands in Our Way

When moments of conflict and tension occur between partners, harshness or disinterest may appear on the surface, while underneath either partner may be carrying any of the following fears:

- When you, as my partner, are angry, sad, or anxious about me, I either have to change your mind, distract you, defend myself, or lay low until it blows over. If I can't do one of these things, I will lose you, or me, or both.
- If I shift my focus and care to you, I have to let go of me.
- If I give too much, I will lose ground.

Additionally, what one partner considers to be a perfectly logical attempt to help the situation often falls flat for the other.

Under stress and with these fears, even the most caring, compassionate, and open-minded people can shift into a mindset of right-versus-wrong, good-versus-bad, and me-versus-you.

In these moments, the essence of *we* is shielded from view. When we add the impact of any traumatic or stressful events experienced by one or both partners, the potential for disconnection becomes even more understandable. As shared by Bessel van der Kolk in *The Body Keeps the Score*, "Traumatized people are afraid of conflict. They fear losing control and ending up on the losing side once again."

From that fear, partners often say, think, and do things that harm the relationship, like defending, criticizing, or avoiding. Many couples have a way to talk through the inevitable disruptions that arise; but when the interactions repeat without resolution, monstrous negative cycles can develop that are difficult to reverse without help.

Trauma and couples therapies—such as highly researched and evidence-based Eye Movement Desensitization and Reprocessing (EMDR) for trauma and Emotionally Focused Therapy (EFT) for couples, as well as many other therapies and healing modalities—are designed to remove any blocks standing in the way of secure relating. Once blocks are removed, some partners step right into the new positive way of being together as a couple, while some benefit from additional skills and coaching.

Once a feeling of togetherness returns for couples in our sessions, often the next question they ask is: "How do we do this at home?"

Mad Libs for Your Relationship

"Do you have scripts? I need scripts. I'm busy... just tell me what to say!"

—Kristina Biondolillo

Kristina Biondolillo, a busy mother, CCP at Cleveland Clinic, and executive director of Marilyn's Voice, a nonprofit animal rescue, is clear about what she needs and what she doesn't. She doesn't need convincing that balanced relating is a good idea. Like many others, she wants to know the fewest possible words to start her down the right track when emotions are high and the moment is precious.

Naturally, words alone will feel incomplete without a genuine and congruent match of emotion, which is easiest to embody when you're not anxious about whether or not you can remember a reliable path forward. This book is designed to give you that head start, to help you create integrity with your AWE (Actions, Words, and Energy) by helping you identify and address blocks, giving you a little structure and lots of room to be your authentic selves.

Is This Book for You?

When couples come for counseling, they often don't know if they need therapy to work through the impact of past events, coaching to learn and practice new skills with each other, or both. Most often, they know they want better communication. Either their relationship is good and they've come to make it better, or they're telling me something hurts and they just can't get what they want for themselves, as they reveal their longing for something more. They are wives, husbands, boyfriends, girlfriends, significant others, those who have never been married, and those who are giving partnership another try.

This book is for people who are willing to risk opening themselves, even if just a little, to see what might be possible. These pages, intended to be explored by partners reading separately or together, include stories, dialogue, ideas, coaching steps called Moves, and two illustrated characters who show up to highlight concepts and help us build compassion for the sometimes-confusing things we do to love and be loved.

Throughout the book, I will draw upon:

- My training as a therapist specializing in trauma and couples therapies;
- Thousands of hours working with clients intensively, mostly in three-hour sessions;
- Interviews with over seventy-five individuals and couples who are not my clients; and
- The wisdom of experts and artists from the fields of counseling, psychology, body-oriented therapies, sports, and the arts.

We humans espouse many ideal intentions, yet in the daily living of our relationships we're going to skip steps, get hijacked by our emotional brains, and find ourselves offtrack as many times as not. When that happens, how do we return to what we know?

As the late poet and philosopher John O'Donohue reminds us of our natural world:

"The sun never rises on the same landscape twice."

Similarly, we, our life stages, and our situations are ever changing. This book is my invitation for you to shine loving care and attention on the unfolding beauty of the home you are and can become for each other.

PART I

THE SPOTLIGHT
OF LOVE

CHAPTER 1

SPOTLIGHT OVERVIEW

Are you seeking guidance to make sure you and your partner are there for each other long-term?

Do you ever experience conflict that includes the same kinds of reactions over and over?

* * *

Often when negative cycles are in the mix, one or both partners start doing very human and remarkably unhelpful things, such as:

Defending,

"I WAS JUST..."

criticizing,

avoiding the problem,

or avoiding altogether.

Perhaps this dynamic feels familiar: You usually have compassion for each other and solve problems effectively, but when your partner is angry, sad, shut down, or anxious about you, maybe you automatically try to:

Change your partner's mind,

defend yourself,

distract them,

or lay low until it blows over.

We've all been in these moments, and deep down we know these strategies don't help because it's how we respond and feel responded to that matters.

Although spotlights are sometimes thought of as an interrogation device or indicate uncomfortable attention in front of a crowd, there is another type of spotlight that is neither harsh nor demanding.

The Spotlight of Love

Imagine an invisible spotlight dangles at the-ready between you and your partner wherever you go. This light shines loving care and attention and has the potential to be a deeply inspiring, soothing, and healing force. We may crave, deflect, hide from, or barely recognize this light, or the glow may feel very comfortable and easily shared. Either way, such love is a powerful beam we want to invite and welcome.

For the health and happiness of the relationship, each partner needs time in the other's focused loving care (a.k.a. the Spotlight), yet there are many ways in which we all struggle to give and receive this light. In the chapters of Part I, we are going to slow things down and explore what it means to hold the beam steady and to stand in its glow.

Keeping Both Partners in the Game

The Spotlight model includes a set of skills that can be challenging to use when someone close to you is having a difficult feeling, and especially so when the complaint or difficult feeling is about you. When the one we love attributes their unhappiness to us, it can be really hard to hear—so hard that, rather than being comforting with our words and our presence, we might:

- Defend ourselves, which often starts with, "Well, I meant…"
- Blame ourselves in a collapsing way, like, "You're right… I'm no good."
- Blame the other person, as in, "Why do you always…?" or
- Avoid the other person altogether.

We react as though some part of us thinks we can ignore the problem and hope it goes away, talk our partner out of the complaint or difficult feeling, or distract and grab their attention by suddenly having a greater need than they do. These strategies don't work because they take the Spotlight away from the person who raised the concern in the first place.

If you have a concern, you deserve loving care and attention, and if your significant other raises a concern, they deserve that care and attention too. It's like you're playing a game of relational ping-pong with the goal of seeing how many consecutive volleys you can tally together. Since the goal is to keep both of you in the game, you don't just watch the ball go by, smash it at your partner, or send it sailing over their head. Instead, you want to receive, make contact, and give something back to keep the process alive.

If your relationship becomes one-sided and the Spotlight is shining in one direction a lot more than the other, we'll tackle that dynamic together in later chapters. For now, we want to ensure the person who has raised the concern or difficult feeling gets the care they need from you. They are coming to you because you matter so much, and you want to be of help for them because they matter so much (Lange 2021).

Spotlight Moves

The steps of the model are called **Moves**. The Moves provide structure for slowing down aspects of an interaction. When using the Moves, you find yourself in one of two roles:

- The role of **Giving**, from which you shine the care and attention of the Spotlight on your partner for the duration of the four giving Moves; or
- The role of **Receiving**, from which you receive the care and attention of your partner. In this role, you are also **Revealing** your inner world of feelings and thoughts along the way.

Spotlight Moves (Generous Giving)

Pause and play buttons are available as well. You'll use pause frequently and intentionally to slow down interactions. The Spotlight provides clarity as well as a path toward emotional safety, which is present when you trust you can share your authentic, unfolding self with your partner. For our purposes, play isn't about starting the action again. As safety develops, repeated moments of play create the neural pathways for a new or reclaimed baseline of playfulness (Gordon 2014). Once partners feel invited, validated, and cared for, the play button often turns itself on.

The Giving role asks a lot of you. It asks you to hold onto yourself emotionally, which means you are able to manage any inner emotional distress you have, while also reaching for your partner via the giving Moves.

This holding and reaching can be a challenging combination. Research reveals that during conflict, regardless of what might be visible on the outside, partners can become physiologically *activated* or *flooded* in such a way that their heart rates rise, their blood oxygen levels fall, and they release stress hormones such as adrenaline and cortisol—all of which severely limit their ability to listen, empathize, and respond thoughtfully (Gottman and Gottman, 2018).

Spotlight Moves (Receiving/Revealing)

The Receiving/Revealing role also asks much of you, to state whether or not you can receive your partner's care and attention without deflecting or batting it away. We have understandable reasons for doing things like defending ourselves or deflecting attention. We want to invite these reasons and reactions into the Spotlight as well.

While in this role, you are invited to reveal vulnerable feelings and insecurities rather than lashing out or shutting down.

When you and your partner first notice you've become disconnected, you can triage your situation by asking each other, "Who gets the Spotlight first?" After you both go through the Moves of your current role, you then trade places, which is an important part of creating a healthy flow of giving and receiving.

Matching Words and Emotional Energy

From the Giving role, as you work to manage your own thoughts and feelings so you can reach for your partner, you'll be tapping into the parts of you that genuinely mean what you're saying.

For instance, anyone with a willingness to engage with the Spotlight likely has some part of them that is genuinely glad to be told about feelings—even difficult ones. See if you can find the genuinely grateful part of yourself before speaking. The words of the first Move will help you get there, as you'll see in the next chapter. You can also close your eyes and picture a positive moment with your partner. Once you're vividly reliving the moment, let the good feelings peak, and then see if you can access your natural curiosity and caring.

Sometimes a partner can't find the generously giving part of themself until they receive the Spotlight first, even if only for a few minutes. Once you become fluid with the Moves, you will be able to notice what roles you are currently in and signal when you are switching back and forth.

You, Me, and We

According to philosopher Martin Buber, "When two people actively and authentically engage each other in the here and now and truly *show up* to one another [...] a new relational dimension [called] *the between* becomes manifest." The relationship becomes greater than the individual contributions in ways that couldn't have been planned or predicted (Martin and Cowan, 2019).

I think of the Spotlight as the ever-present *between* Buber describes.

In an ideal world, the love of *the between* would shine on everyone, all the time, without fail. However, in our lived experiences, we get reactive—whether we show it outwardly or not. This means we need a way to consciously direct the ever-present Spotlight to only one partner at a time.

How Did That Go?

When we're having a strong emotional reaction and perceive that our partner is not on our side, our thinking can become rigid, which is entirely understandable given our human wiring for threat. We forget we are also wired for connection and have Moves available to help us slow things down and begin to calm our own and each other's nervous systems. One of the benefits of these practical Spotlight Moves is they help us understand where we're stuck. (Recognizing precisely where the "stuck points" are via the Clarity Assessment questions in Chapter 9 will help you know where to focus for reconnection.)

Very few couples breeze right through the Spotlight Moves the first time. In close relationships, stuff comes up. We get hooked into reactive patterns and habits. Just like becoming proficient in a sport, dance, or any activity you love, this endeavor also takes a lot of practice.

When you practice the Moves, the time spent experiencing disconnection due to a you-versus-me dynamic shortens, becomes less frequent, and is experienced with less distress, while the time of connection and a sense of togetherness expands.

Balance becomes balancing as you develop a strong and flexible foundation that can hold you through your growth and changes.

No Buts About It

At each stage of relationship, holding onto yourself *and* reaching toward your partner involves art, skill, intuition, and practice. The language we use also matters greatly. Perhaps the most important word we'll use in this book can be found in the next three letters:

When used in place of *but*, the word *and* allows two seemingly competing ideas to be held side by side. Where the word *but* minimizes everything that came before, the word *and* expands us beyond dualistic thinking. When we trade *but* for *and*, we create the space for ideas to unfold and be explored. If this substitution becomes a habit, we can change the way we think.

Language literally changes our neurobiology, as evidenced by the research of Andrew Newberg, MD, and Mark Robert Waldman. In their book, *Words Can Change Your Brain*, they write:

"A single word has the power to influence the expression of genes that regulate physical and emotional stress."

Consider these examples:

- "I care about what you're saying, *but* I have to go to work."
- "I feel anxious with her, *but* she's family."

In the first example, the speaker minimizes what's being said to them. In the second, the speaker dismisses their own experience. Minimizing and dismissing are found in me-versus-you relationships. When we allow for all to be present (e.g., "I care about what you're saying, *and* I have to go to work") there is often a pause and, with that held beat, a new possibility.

Another significant aspect of the word *and* is that you can add as many statements as you like, which can be very helpful when speaking from your heart in the moment. For example:

"I feel anxious with her,
and
she's family,
and
she pushes my buttons,
and
I love her dearly."

All these ideas need to be present to communicate the fullness of the message.

The word *and* creates a small shift with only a few letters. This is a language of paradox that allows us to hold things together, one in each hand and both in each heart. The word *and* is also a central element to the question we explore throughout this book:

How do I hold onto me **and** reach for you?

*   *   *

CHAPTER 2

GENEROUS GIVING (MOVES 1 AND 2)

"I can't believe you did it again."

* * *

Heated moments can lead to snide comments or conde-scending attitudes. Since reactivity happens, we need a way to consciously direct the Spotlight of Love to one partner and then the other. Through this authentic exchange, we are far more capable of generous giving and courageous receiving/revealing than we might have known possible.

As a reminder, the Spotlight has two roles:

- Receiving/Revealing—the role of the partner who is actively receiving the love and care being shined upon them while also revealing their inner world with as much vulnerability as possible; and

- Giving—the role of the partner who is holding the Spotlight steady.

The way we reflect the qualities and experiences of another person is one of the privileges of loving. As psychologist, meditation teacher, and author Tara Brach reminds us in her book *Radical Acceptance:*

"Our trust in our own basic goodness emerges from the clear and deep mirroring of others."

Spotlight giving holds up a positive mirror so your loved one's basic goodness can come forth in your presence.

The giving Moves can be challenging in practice. When your partner is perceived as being inaccessible or unresponsive (e.g., angry, disappointed, or shut down toward you) then emotions such as fear, anger, sadness, or confusion can override other information you have in the moment. This means you might react to your partner's reactions, momentarily forgetting what you know about connection.

Remembering what you know is easier when you:

- Have established Moves (in the form of sentence starters, which we'll discuss shortly) to rely upon;
- Have an experience of what it's like to be in the Receiving/Revealing role; and
- Trust that your thoughts and feelings will receive attention when the Spotlight shifts back to you.

Couples often report initial moments of conflict similar to the one found below in "The Story of the Dishes." In this story, imagine yourself in the role of the Giving partner. The partners depicted here successfully navigate every key moment. Remember few, if any, couples will be able to do this the first time through! I share in this way to show you what is possible. Secure relationships, the ones where you know you can count on each other, are about being good enough. They don't demand perfection.

The Story of the Dishes

It all begins with some backward plates.

One day you're in the kitchen together and your partner, standing by the dishwasher, says, "I can't believe you did it again. The dishes. Go. Like. This." Exaggerated arm movements match the angry tone and emphasis on each word.

If we pause right here, you (like any of us) might have the impulse to defend yourself, blame your partner for acting that way, try to talk them out of their feelings, or avoid the whole thing and hope this tense moment goes away.

However, since we're flirting with what's possible, let's look at this situation from the perspective of being secure within yourself. Essentially, this means you're able to handle any tension you might be feeling without ramping up the intensity or avoiding. You're able to think in terms of the big picture, set yourself aside for an amount of time, and keep the focus on your partner. You have a strong enough sense that you're good and lovable, and a strong enough trust that your partner will swing the loving Spotlight back to you later if you have feelings about this that need attention.

I'm not suggesting you suppress your feelings such that they're never heard from again. You're just setting them aside for now because you can. And if you can't, don't worry. We will address that in upcoming chapters.

When couples become disconnected, both might feel reactive at the same time. In these moments a triage is needed. This is when you look at each other and say, "Okay, who gets the Spotlight first?" and decide based on who raised the concern and who is most able to be in the Giving role in that moment. For now, imagine you're able to calm yourself enough to be in the role of generous Giving. Here are the Moves to start you down the path of reconnection:

MOVE 1:
"I'M SO GLAD YOU TOLD ME..."

This Move is always the same. Even if your partner has just tossed a relational harpoon or hand grenade your way, you are going to be grateful and inviting with your AWE. You've practiced this Move, and you're ready.

When your partner says, "I can't believe you did it again," about the dishes, you become the Giving partner, the one who lovingly and courageously holds the Spotlight as you say, "I'm so glad you told me." You are sending the clear message that you are grateful to be learning about your partner.

Remember, this person going on about the dishes is the one you love. They are your partner, your spouse, your girl-friend, or your boyfriend, and they are sharing their inner world with you. Even if what they're saying is that they're stratospherically mad at you right now, what a gift that is! They're letting you in.

Sometimes, even the kindest and most loving people initially say, "I *don't* want to know about this! I want this feeling/expression/problem to go away!" When we pause and welcome this reluctance, then the part that *does* want to know usually comes to the forefront. If you honestly can't find any part of you that wants to know about your partner's inner world, then take a good look at this as soon as you can.

Let's say for now that even if you might be managing some stress, deep down you are also grateful your partner told you.

The Moves are here as reminders to start you down the right conversational path. Just like a quarterback would call a play, an improviser would open a scene, and a dance partner would take the lead, you are showing up to say, "I'm here. I know the first Move!"

MOVE 2:

"OF COURSE, YOU FEEL _____"

The second Move validates the feeling. Feelings aren't intrin-sically good or bad. We think of them that way because we assign meaning to them. I will call some feelings *difficult* because they are the ones most often associated with a negative meaning. These difficult feelings are typically some flavor of sad, mad, scared, worried, anxious, or numbed out and foggy.

Validating your partner's positive feelings is just as vital as being with their negative ones. Validating the feeling doesn't necessarily mean you agree with the thinking. For this Move, focus on what your partner is feeling. Feelings are real and deserve your care.

- If your partner has already revealed their feeling (e.g., "I'm angry"), then you can validate that: "Of course you're angry!"
- If your partner tends to know how they feel and can reveal that feeling to you, then asking, "How do you feel?" is a great way to discover which feeling to validate. Maybe they aren't angry or don't identify with the word *anger* but instead want you to hear they are overwhelmed or frustrated.
- If your partner tends to not vulnerably reveal feelings, then your calm presence and a gentle, validating guess can be helpful (e.g., "It makes sense if you're frustrated. Is that it?"). Be open to using their words if they redirect you.

You may be thinking, "But I want to fix it!" The Spotlight Moves prevent the tempting rush to fix a situation. Although solutions are a good and necessary part of life, when we rush to them habitually, often one or both people are left feeling unheard or misunderstood.

Validating a feeling can seem counterintuitive to someone who firmly believes they know what is causing the distress and wants to fix the problem. The truth of this tension between validation and problem-solving is evidenced by the nearly twenty-three million views of a two-minute YouTube video called, "It's Not About the Nail," in which one partner wants emotional validation and the other wants to move forward with what appears to be the obvious solution to the humorous dilemma. Once feelings are validated, most people find it easier to include other strategies.

After validating, pause.

Pause.

Maybe even pause some more.

When we slow things down, more can be revealed.

The Power of the Pause

When our partner is upset and we genuinely want to help, we sometimes overwork because we think we need to do more than necessary. We also overdo it as a result of our own anxiety.

Conversely, we might freeze, which looks like underworking. Here, the pause can help bring you back to yourself and then to your partner. Both overworking and underworking are emotional reactions that deserve attention. Future chapters will offer ideas for what might be helpful if this is happening for you.

Again, Move 2 is, "Of course you're angry!" or "It makes sense that you're angry!" followed by a pause.

While pausing, try to connect emotionally rather than staying in your head. Use your eyes and expressions. The key to validating well is matching the emotional energy coming your way without dodging, hiding, shrinking, or going into fix-it mode. For example, if your partner is angry, don't deliver a calm, monotone, "Oh, you're angry." This will probably be rejected because it's a mismatch of energy.

You might also risk disconnection if you say in a calm voice, "Oh, you're angry. That's because you're nervous." This would be both a mismatch of emotional energy and you telling them why they're angry. Even if you're right, they might not be ready to hear that, and they could experience you as "just not getting it."

You have a better chance of connection if you raise your voice and energy to say, "Of course you're angry!" or "I get it, you're angry!" or "It makes sense that you feel angry!" and then pause.

You are communicating to your partner that you are secure enough to stand with them in their feelings—even if these feelings are directed at you! You are communicating, *I want to know about your anger. I'm interested. I'm glad you're telling me*, which often creates the space to begin a more connected conversation.

If you aren't yet secure enough to keep the Spotlight on your partner, you might feel some shame about that. I know I have felt shame about my Spotlight-grabbing moments, and I see many partners experience the same when they learn about this Move they can't quite make yet. Grabbing the Spotlight from time to time doesn't make you defective; it makes you human.

Being in the same old dilemma then having a new positive connecting experience, and feeling the relief and happiness wash over you knowing you did it together, makes up for a lot of missteps. When it comes to creating secure connection with your partner, just like in baseball, you might frequently strike out. The reward for taking that swing, though, is that when you get a hit (or feel that closeness) you gain the confidence to stay in the game. If you're successful one-third of the time, according to experts in the fields of both human bonding and baseball, you're having a great year.

Languaging

Memorizing the sentence starter, "Of course you feel _____" sets you on the path of energetically being with your partner in their feeling. With that same energy, you can use different words, such as, "It makes sense that you feel _____."

Once you both know the energy and intent are trusted between the two of you, and that neither of you will try to talk the other out of their feelings, then even a simple, "Yeah, you feel _____" will help your partner know you are with them. Your ability to be with them in their feelings will be the soothing element.

Circling Back

When a mutual flow of energy exists, we can always circle back with the Moves. For example, in my own life I often miss my opportunity to validate feelings. In the tense moment, I grab the Spotlight and shine the beam on myself. This happened last night with my kids.

They were angry over a racial injustice directed toward one of their friends. I was angry, too, yet rather than validating their anger with an energetic match, I went into problem-solving mode. Not until the next morning did I realize I missed the opportunity to validate and join with them in their feelings. I know intellectually that validating feelings calms nervous systems and expands thinking, yet in my own fear, I skipped a step. Fortunately, I knew I could circle back, as I did later that day.

When we circle back on a regular basis, our relationships become continuing conversations. The Move to validate the feeling becomes its own cycle. As your partner continues to reveal, you can continue to validate and pause as many times as needed. You'll probably be able to tell by your partner's responses if you are getting it, and you can always gently ask, "Is that what you're feeling?"

Are You Here?

Regardless of what's been directed at you in terms of tone, words, or energy, the distressed partner (the one currently in the Receiving/Revealing role) is almost always silently asking, *Are you here with me?* Throughout this interaction, you are communicating, *I am here with you.*

While in the Giving role, you are holding the beam steady and you're tracking your partner, which is different from being your partner. They may have made two turns, crossed a stream, and entered a foggy valley in the last two minutes. Be compassionate with yourself. You're listening and following as best you can, and there will be help for you from your partner once we get to the Revealing/Receiving role in later chapters.

Summary

As a reminder, the Spotlight giving Moves covered so far are:

- "I'm so glad you told me!"
- "Of course you feel _____."

 In Which Direction Lies Your Growth?

Since any term, skill, or Move is relative and exists along a continuum, we will include in our thinking directions of growth for you as an individual as well as for your relationship. Identifying an area of growth doesn't necessarily mean striving to improve on a weakness. Partners often have areas of strength and gifts that they may have trouble accessing in their primary relationship. Consider your directions of growth as expanding on innate gifts you already have and learning how you might complement each other in these areas.

- Once you have the opportunity to experiment with the Moves, can you access the genuinely grateful part of you by saying, "I'm so glad you told me," when your partner is sharing a dissatisfaction?
- Validating feelings with "Of course you feel _____" can take some practice. I encourage you to use this phrase with several people in your life until it becomes comfortable and readily available for you when you need it.
- How do you feel about circling back? Is that a comforting thought, or does it make your palms sweat?

- As you imagine being the Giving partner in "The Story of the Dishes," what directions of growth would feel most natural for you, and how might you expand further into your own nature?

CHAPTER 3

GENEROUS GIVING (MOVES 3 AND 4)

"I feel like you don't care about me when you load the dishes this way."

Uh-oh. How do I respond to that?

✳ ✳ ✳

In the previous chapter, you learned the first two Spotlight Moves of generous giving. Now you are bravely venturing into joining with your partner in their thoughts and feelings. This joining greatly reduces the fear of being on opposite sides. As UVA professor Jim Coan states:

"We seek signals from each other that we are together. When we lack those signals, our bodies go into a state of alarm that triggers a stress response."

Conversely, receiving signals that we are together, even when difficult emotions are present, elicits a sense of warmth, calm, and security. Our capacities for stress are greater when we feel united.

As a reminder, the first two Moves of the previous chapter are: "I'm so glad you told me," and "Of course you feel _____." This next one is a bonus. If you'd like to stretch, give it a try. If you're not feeling all that stretchy right now, then waiting for the next time makes sense!

(BONUS MOVE:)

"THE MEANING YOU MAKE IS _____"

Let's say your validation via Move 2 was soothing for your partner. They soften a little and then reveal, "I feel like you don't care about me when you load the dishes this way."

In this instance, you can expand into new territory by reflecting the thought they are having, which would sound like, "Oh, I see, the meaning you make or the thought you have is that I don't care about *you*."

As you read this, you might be thinking, *But it doesn't make sense that they would think or feel this way! How can I say this if it doesn't make sense?*

Understanding your partner's reactions do make sense on some level is important. We are all capable of sounding irrational or shutting down. When we follow the wound or insecurity to the root, this current reaction does make sense. Your partner could be experiencing something that looks, sounds, or feels like something that hurt them in the past, and that creates a cascade of feelings, thoughts, and physiological responses similar to the original experience.

As one woman shared:

> I thought trauma was the terrible thing that happened to you, rather than what happens inside of you when you don't receive a loving and empathetic response following a terrible event.
>
> Understanding what trauma is changed my relationship to the word, which, frankly, had begun to annoy me [due to its ubiquity], and opened up a much greater sense of compassion and understanding about my own trauma—and that of others—at the individual, cultural, and collective levels. It also helped me understand why trauma-informed *everything* could have a profound effect on how we relate to one another.
>
> It's easier to be with someone else's trauma knowing that I have an opportunity to be a presence for them in a way they didn't receive at an earlier time.

You have an opportunity to be the loving presence she describes. In many instances, by making these Spotlight Moves you are validating your partner's *limbic logic*, which comes from the part of their brain that has fight, flight, freeze, or tend-and-befriend reactions.

Returning to our story with the dishes, you might say, "Oh. It makes sense. When I don't load the dishes the way you've asked, you feel angry, and the meaning you make is that I don't care about you."

Pause, and gently ask, "Is that it?"

Ask your questions or make your guesses tentatively. You are exploring this together.

Even if you cognitively disagree with your partner's conclusion, validating their feelings and reflecting the understood meaning helps create the conditions for the feelings and beliefs to transform. You are giving your partner and your relationship the radiant gift of your caring responsiveness. Feelings are real, even if either or both of you disagree with the meaning one partner makes or the magnitude one partner places on that meaning.

Once the feeling is acknowledged skillfully and the person feels understood and met where they are, often he or she will transform the belief naturally.

Beliefs Gone Global

Under stress, we can go global with our assumptions (e.g., "If you don't put the dishes the right way, that means you don't care about me *at all!*"). As the Giving partner, it can be a big relief to understand that the global message "You don't care about me at all" is likely a fear created by reactivity in the moment. You don't need to talk your partner out of that fear. As you practice the Moves, their relationship to the fear will likely change over time.

And what if the fear doesn't transform and your partner still thinks you're a rat for turning the dishes the wrong way? Well—this might sound easy for me to say, but that's okay too. You're okay. In a healthy or becoming-healthy relationship, the Spotlight is going to swing back to you. With this knowledge, it's easier to persevere with validating feelings and getting closer to the core meaning for your partner. When we slow things down, get curious, and find comfort with circling back, we have time for it all.

MOVE 3:

"DO YOU KNOW
WHAT YOU NEED?"

The next Move is: "Do you know what you need?" You can add, "It's okay if you don't."

You're gently exploring how to help rather than interrogating for an answer. The difference in these two can be a game changer. You're helping your partner know what would feel supportive to them, which is different from the need to be a good rule follower who asks the right questions.

Each partner's list of needs will be unique. Think of this as a menu of options. As the Giving partner, you want to learn what's on your partner's menu. Of course, they will want different things at different times, and a robust Menu gives you the flexibility to enjoy a delicious feast together.

This is a menu about what your partner needs from you right now in order to feel your connection again. As the Giving partner, you are giving what you are able. If what your partner needs right now is problem-solving, then you can consciously talk about the future and might need to shift the Spotlight back and forth to create a plan that works for you both. Thoughts on negotiating are presented in Chapter 13.

While learning the Spotlight, I recommend that both partner menus include plenty of comforting options for the present moment. The following are examples of partner menus:

Menu 1
- Extra validation
- Holding hands or sitting close
- Telling me about a time you felt the same way
- Telling me what you were thinking/feeling so I can understand (Note: This requires switching the Spotlight temporarily.)

Menu 2
- Brainstorming new ideas
- Problem solving
- Saying "Grrr" together
- Enjoying quiet connection

In the example with the dishes, when you ask your partner, "What do you need right now?" they might respond, "Can you just wrap your arms around me for a few minutes?" If your partner is home with kids all day, they might say, "You get so much positive feedback for your great ideas at work. Can you remind me that what I'm doing is really important too?" They may say instead, "If we don't do the dishes this way, it feels like more chaos. I'd love some help thinking of ways to de-stress." What becomes clear in any of these responses is:

It's not about the dishes!

This moment is about the feelings and beliefs underlying your partner's stress and the opportunity to be of comfort with your touch, your words, and your willingness to collaborate.

MOVE 4:
"IS THERE
ANYTHING ELSE
ABOUT THIS?"

At this point, you as the Giving partner have made so many terrific relational Moves. You have gratefully appreciated your partner's complaint, validated their feelings, and reflected the meaning they were making from their upset. You have discovered what they need from you in this moment, and you were able to give generously. Now, it's time for the last giving Move: "Is there anything else about this?"

This question is closely aligned with the first grateful and inviting Move, "I'm so glad you told me." Since awareness unfolds over time, there might be something else about this same situation your partner wants to reveal. If so, you can either return to the Moves now with this new detail, or you can both decide to return to it later. Simply asking the question is part of creating an environment where you can thrive together.

The Role of the Receiving/Revealing Partner

In this everything-goes-well example, you imagined yourself as the Giving partner, able to manage your discomfort and direct the Spotlight's loving attention. At the same time, your partner was also making some pretty amazing Moves to reveal their inner world and receive your care and attention. Sure, they began with some exaggerated arm movements and blame about the dishes, and then they responded to your responsiveness.

> The goal isn't that we never have difficult feelings. The aim is to invite these feelings into the loving Spotlight.

Continuing with our story, let's say your partner, who came to you with the complaint about the dishes, feels better and doesn't need anything else from you about this. Now it's time to swing the Spotlight to you. Some partners might discount their feelings or not even notice them and be reluctant to shift into the Receiving role, yet I encourage each of you to practice giving *and* receiving. Spending time in both roles helps create partnership and balance.

Either your partner could initiate the switch by asking, "What was it like for you when I yelled about the dishes?" or you can ask for the Spotlight. In fact, it's important that you're able to make that request, which could sound something like, "Can I share what I felt when you brought up the dishes?" Also, either of you could simply say, "Let's switch."

Now, imagine yourself in the role of the Receiving/Revealing partner.

From Your New Vantage Point

Perhaps you, as the Receiver/Revealer, say, "When I saw your face and heard you slamming dishes, I thought, *Oh no*, and I felt frozen at first. I know I usually shut down when you're upset, but I kept telling myself, *It's okay, I can do this*. Not turning away was really hard."

Your partner says something inviting, such as, "I'm so glad you told me," and the positive cycle starts again.

Your partner: "Of course you felt frozen. That must have been kind of scary." Gently, "Is that right?"

Pause here.

You: "Exactly. I didn't realize how scared I get."

Your partner: "Do you know what meaning you're making or what you are saying to yourself when you get scared?"

You: "That I just can't get it right—and then I get worried."

Your partner: "Oh yeah, that makes sense. You start to worry that you can't get it right when you're scared."

You: "Yeah."

Your partner gently asks: "Do you know what you need?"

You: "Yes. Will you remind me that you're happy with me, you know, as a person, and that we'll figure these things out?"

Their embrace, resonating over the softly spoken words, says it all.

What If My Partner Doesn't Know What They Feel?

Identifying feelings will be much easier for some than others. If your partner says, "I don't know what I feel," believe them. They are learning how. Likewise, if your partner talks about the feeling more than *feeling* the feeling in the moment with you, be patient with this as well.

As trust and emotional safety develop and you continue practicing, identifying and feeling emotions while you're together becomes easier. You are helping each other rediscover all that's been covered up due to trauma and conditioning.

What If My Partner Doesn't Know What They Need?

Identifying what would be comforting in the present moment isn't always as easy as it might sound. If your partner doesn't know what they need right now, you can gently offer from their menu of options. You might be calmer and clearer than they are, so your mind is freer to think of things. At the same time, it's not your responsibility to know something they don't know themselves.

Maintaining a spirit of collaboration, you might gently offer, "We could stay quiet together," following this with a pause.

If offered tentatively and with pauses, your partner might enjoy additional suggestions, such as, "I'm happy to listen more if you want to talk," or "I could brainstorm with you."

Push that play button, too, if the timing feels right. Suggest, "I could share the bazillion moments when I've felt overwhelmed," "We can 'Grrr' together about how frustrating our adorable children can be," "I could hold you," or "Take your time. I'm here."

As your partner relaxes further, you can have a different conversation. As the two of you reconnect, your brains release neurochemicals called vasopressin and oxytocin.

'These nurture your bond and create room for playfulness, exposing how, when we ramp up the intensity or turn away, what we really want is to be loved and lovable in each other's eyes.

The next chapter explores ways to learn from the challenges many of us face when asked to make these giving Moves.

Summary

As a reminder, the Spotlight giving Moves are:

- "I'm so glad you told me!"
- "Of course you feel _____."
- "The meaning you make is _____."
- "What do you need?"
- "Is there anything else about this?"

When your partner's reactions touch and activate your own, you might be tempted to grab the loving Spotlight and shine it on yourself out of defense and your own need for care. Being able to calm yourself inside and keep the Spotlight on your partner while trusting it will swing back to you is not easy. Let's move forward to address blocks, offer strategies, and wrestle with common confusions.

In Which Direction Lies Your Growth?

- Consider your areas of growth as expanding on gifts you already have. As you reflect on your giving Moves, which feels the easiest for you? Where might you want to stretch?
- What topics in your relationship might benefit from a Spotlight conversation?
- As you imagine being the Giving partner, what intentions or healing are you drawn toward?

CHAPTER 4

CHALLENGES OF GENEROUS GIVING

In the world of improvisational comedy, not *everything* is made-up. There are general structures for a student of the art to study. Within these structures, everything is improvised. Players are generously listening for and following each other in ways that support the scene.

Similarly, the Spotlight provides a structure in which each partner generously gives, vulnerably reveals, and courageously receives loving care—except when they don't. And sometimes, they won't. At that point, they arrive at the opportunity to watch and listen for what will happen next.

To learn more about the application of improv skills to our Spotlight giving, I interviewed Pam Victor, Head of Happiness (also president and founder) at Happier Valley Comedy in Western Massachusetts. As I heard Pam's values and practices for her theater, I began to think we'd been leading parallel lives as enthusiastic coaches for our clients and students. Her teaching fundamentals and mindsets include:

- You have everything you need to be a good improviser, *and* there are some structures to learn.
- Improv is acceptance of reality in the moment and the agreement to move forward together with joy and ease.
- Keep practicing. It's all about patience, persistence, and putting in the time.
- Let's talk about your fears. We can't help what we don't know about.
- One good show makes up for a lot of bad ones.
- Embrace fucking it up. Mastery is a myth.

Of course, one big difference between an improv scene partner and your romantic partner is your romantic partner is most often the primary person in your life. You and your loved one are not saying goodbye when the show is over because your relational show goes on and your scenes together are far-reaching. These very facts can ramp up the intensity, which also makes the in-the-moment skills of improv extra valuable.

Navigating Inner Dialogues

Imagine a moment when your partner needed the Spotlight and you weren't able to resist shining the light back on yourself. Once you have this moment in your mind, see if any of these initial thoughts or challenges fit, even if you weren't aware of them at the time:

- Challenge 1: I don't know what to do.
- Challenge 2: I know what to do, yet some part of me doesn't want to give to you generously right now.

- Challenge 3: (After lashing out or shutting down) I knew what to do. Why couldn't I do it?
- Challenge 4: Oh no, I messed up. Now it's too late.
- Challenge 5: I know what to do. I'm doing it, and it doesn't seem to be helping.

Challenge 1: I Don't Know What to Do

You're a willing partner who hasn't yet learned about Spotlight giving and receiving. Among the challenges, this one has the most straightforward recommendations: Learn, memorize, and practice the Moves.

MOVE 1: "I'm so glad you told me."
MOVE 2: "Of course, you feel _____"
(BONUS: "The meaning you make is _____")
MOVE 3: "What do you need?"
MOVE 4: "Is there anything else about this?"

This is the structure from which you begin. You won't be able to tell if you have an emotional block to implementing the Moves until you know what the Moves are and you're able to recall them in a calm moment.

As one woman shared, "I thought I *was* validating his feelings. I guess I didn't really know what the term meant."

A man I spoke with had a different concern about validation: "I thought this validating feelings approach would mean we'd be stuck in [the feelings] forever. Seems like it really helped her, though. I guess I'm that way too. I usually don't like to be given advice about what to do when I just want her to see how I feel."

Experience is such a wonderful teacher in this way. I encourage you to run an experiment with the giving Moves and observe the outcome within yourself and among your people.

Challenge 2: I Know What to Do, Yet Some Part of Me Doesn't Want to Give to You Generously Right Now

This book is written for the willing partner, yet this challenge sounds like unwillingness. The distinction resides in the above phrase: *some part of me*. We all have different parts of us which are aspects to our personalities that have varying needs, wants, thoughts, and feelings. You've probably experienced conflicting parts of yourself many times.

Say part of you wants to visit your family for the holiday, while another part secretly dreads the time because, for some reason, you just can't speak up there. You respond enthusiastically, "Yes, I'll be there!" knowing you usually arrive and quickly feel weighed down. The enthusiasm is real, as is the dread.

Learning to honor our competing needs makes choosing our best strategies more possible. As Deany Laliotis, founder of The Center for Excellence in EMDR Therapy, teaches:

"Honor the need. Challenge the strategy."

Being a willing partner means the conscious adult part of you has decided to approach your relationship with willingness. Still, some other part might come through with a strong "No!" in the moment you are called on to be in the Giving role.

A new strategy is needed here, although not the often-prescribed directive to simply "Give more." Instead, I suggest a mindset shift toward the part of you that needs to know you have enough emotional safety to make the reach for your partner. As was shared with me by a therapist years ago:

Your compassion is incomplete if it doesn't include yourself.

Fears, conscious or not, tend to block one's ability to be genuinely grateful and giving. As you read through the list of thoughts and fears below, I invite you to pause and notice if any of them apply to you as you imagine shining the Spotlight on your partner:

- Part of me is afraid this feeling you're having (sad, mad, scared, etc.) will get more intense or happen more often, and I won't be able to handle it.
- Part of me is afraid if I welcome your feeling, I will lose ground. I will give to you, yet again, and you will never appreciate me. I resent you for all the times you left me hanging.
- Part of me doesn't really know if I want our relationship to work. I'm ambivalent. If I care and empathize with you, I might not be able to set the boundary I need to protect myself.

- Part of me thinks this feeling stuff is all unnecessary. It makes me uncomfortable.
- When you're sad, mad, or anxious about something I did, part of me is scared you won't want me anymore.
- Part of me is afraid if I don't respond to you *correctly* right now, I will disappoint you, and I can't stand to disappoint you.
- Part of me resents you. You started this whole mess, and now I need to give you the Spotlight? I'm angry and afraid it will never come back to me.
- If I'm really honest with myself, I'm better at talking *about* feelings than actually feeling them in the moment. I love emotion, and part of me is really scared of conflict.
- Part of me wants to know your vulnerable sides and part of me doesn't. I want to know you can take care of the stressful things for us because I don't know if I can.

If you notice any of the above fears in yourself and are able to set them aside while focusing on your partner, this is heroic. If you aren't yet able to set your fears aside, you are not alone! Exploring the cause and learning how to make these giving Moves despite the fear might be the most heroic act of all.

We all get distracted, make mistakes, and fail to attune to our partner. What matters is the quickness and quality of the return and repair.

Parts of Us

The giving of loving care and attention when your partner is distressed is ideal in theory, as this likely appeals to many parts of the self most of the time. However, parts of you might vehemently disagree in the moments when your fears or frustrations are activated. When we understand the part of self that is brought to the forefront in these moments, then our fears make so much sense! At the same time, we don't want our inner children—who are likely the ones experiencing these fears—driving the cars of our lives. They are dreadful drivers.

Mindset shifts happen when people learn through direct experience that they are emotionally safe within themselves and with each other. This kind of shift can happen initially with a therapist in individual or couples sessions, a family member, a trusted friend, or with your partner if they are also willing and learning along with you.

As you become more practiced at noticing and regulating your own emotions, you will simultaneously be able to make a quick mental note of what you'd like to reveal later when the Spotlight shifts to you.

One partner explained, "I thought if she could just see my point of view, it would make sense to her. I didn't realize I was pulling the Spotlight back to myself when I explained my reasons."

A Quick Switch

As mentioned previously, an important part of the Spotlight model is the triage that confirms who will be giving and who will be receiving first. While learning the model, the partner who first offers to be in the Giving role frequently discovers they just can't do it without interjecting and pulling the Spotlight back to themselves. This is normal and often easily handled. Simply switch this partner into the Receiving role where they can reveal why it's hard for them to give right now. When they receive validation for the feelings driving their hesitation, then they are often willing and able to resume their position in the Giving role.

Each partner will have the opportunity to give and receive— just not at the same time.

Challenge 3: (After Lashing Out or Shutting Down) I Knew What to Do. Why Couldn't I Do It?

This can be the most frustrating challenge of all. You know the Moves. You sincerely want to be able to practice them with your partner. Yet when the moment arrives, you lose it, shut down, or both. In instances like these, when the emotional brain is sounding the alarm, maybe your focus tightens and you have little or no capacity to have an expansive conversation that can unfold over time. Rational thinking goes astray.

Anyone who has ever said or done something they later regret (which is every one of us) can relate. To make matters worse, we can later feel embarrassed about our reactions. We are willing partners, after all, so *what* was *that* all about?

Maybe a root cause trauma was reactivated. Maybe your mind went blank and you started telling yourself a story that's not true. Maybe your blood sugar just crashed. There could be many reasons. When we hold them gently and with curiosity, the focused repetition of the Moves provides opportunities for these confusing knots to loosen a bit so you get an idea of which strand to follow.

Challenge 4: Oh No, I Messed Up. Now It's Too Late.

This challenging inner dialogue is common, yet within secure and becoming-secure relationships, many opportunities arise to circle back to the point at which you got offtrack.

If you're able to simply say, "Oops, can I back up?" or "Can I try this again?" your willingness will shine through and blaze the trail for your Spotlight giving. At least some part of your partner wants to receive, so they are likely to welcome your refocus on them.

If, however, you've become locked in a mode of competition (e.g., "If I make a mistake, I lose."), then jot a quick mental note of that. Later, when you are in the Revealing role, you might allow yourself to wonder: *Am I telling myself I did something irrevocably wrong, or is my partner saying this? Where is this story coming from?* The fear of having lost is not surprising. We live in a culture of competition, yet a relationship is a collaboration in which you want each other to succeed in your roles. In improv, this is akin to making your scene partner look good.

Part of your agreement together will include letting each other try again. Love and relationships can be messy, and we all goof up in our human attempts to love and be loved. Many couples find relief and connection in the *oops* moments. This is a fantastic opportunity to hit the play button as well.

Using the Spotlight is about embracing the concept of your life together as an ongoing conversation. If "Oh no, it's too late" takes you back to an emotional state of helplessness where you aren't able to be in the Giving role, then I recommend finding a trauma therapist with whom you can address this directly.

How to stay with the moment like an improviser

As Pam Victor says, "We embrace fucking it up! It takes the pressure off. Mastery is elusive. What did you learn? I just keep asking that over and over, 'What did you learn?'" This focus helps her students stay in the scene in ways that support her theater's core values of joy and ease.

We need a way to stay in our Spotlight moments as well. The gentleness and self-compassion we give ourselves matters.

Hold onto yourself. Reach for your partner. Stay in your scene.

Challenge 5: I'm Doing All the Moves, And It Doesn't Seem to Be Helping

You can take a few possible routes for this challenge:

- Keep practicing all the Moves.
- Work on validating feelings in every context you can. Your people will love you for it.
- Pay attention to the emotional energy from which you are speaking. Keep addressing your fear and your coping strategies until your giving is all about love.

As late poet and civil rights activist Maya Angelou reminds us:

"People will forget what you said, people will forget what you did, but people will never forget how you make them feel."

Once you have confidence that you're utilizing the skills, what if your relational pattern still feels stuck and your partner isn't experiencing relief as a result of your efforts? Perhaps your partner is having difficulty receiving.

Giving and receiving are closely linked. Let's get curious about how you and your partner experience Receiving. This, as well as vulnerable revealing, are the topics of our next chapter.

Until Then, Practice Like an Improviser

Pam shares that there's no substitute for "patience, persistence, and putting in the time [...]. One good scene, like three cherries on the slot machine, can carry you for another dozen bad performances."

The Spotlight is an experiential model, which means we're always practicing and learning—not just with our heads but with our emotional and energetic bodies too. We do so by beginning in the old familiar fear, only to be surprised and breakthrough to a new experience: of yourself as capable of giving; of your partner who receives you; and of yourself once again, as you notice how wonderful it feels to have your love received. This is the joy of secure relating. One positive loop can carry you through a lot of missed moments.

Understanding Trauma

The notion that trauma refers strictly to events such as accidents and wartime combat is a misconception. Stressful moments in relationships with our closest people can register with the same intensity as major headline events. Until the underlying experience of trauma is healed, you might react in ways that don't make logical sense to you.

If you aren't able to be in the Giving or Receiving role because you are activated (i.e., triggered) to reexperience a younger part of yourself who acquired wounds in relationships, it makes sense that you wouldn't be able to hold the Spotlight steady when your system is over- or under-activated.

We all have emotional reactions, and some experiences can be difficult to heal fully by yourself. If a reaction only arises for you in a relationship, then a relationship brings up the opportunity for a new positive, healing experience. The particular chemical cocktail of your specific fear might be the only emotional state from which certain thoughts, feelings, and behaviors arise. Likewise, this is the emotional state from which the internal experience of trauma can be healed.

In this book, I recommend holding onto yourself, which involves self-knowledge, self-compassion, and self-acceptance, all of which can be extremely difficult if your trauma reactions are strong and include challenging habits of thinking and behavior.

Bessel van der Kolk, MD writes, "When you're traumatized, it becomes even more difficult to know yourself because trauma is actually *not* the story of what happened a long time ago; trauma is residue that's living inside of you now; trauma lives inside of you in horrible sensations, panic reactions, uptightness, explosions, and impulses. Because trauma lives inside of you, getting to know yourself can be the scariest thing to do. It takes an enormous amount of courage to visit and befriend yourself and to feel what that uptightness is about. Having the courage to let yourself relax and to notice the flow of your body is central for recovery."

For the challenge of trauma-based reactivity, interventions which help disrupt the maladaptive loops of thinking, feeling, physiology, and behavior are recommended, as is looking for a therapist who practices experientially. This person is trained and comfortable working with whatever comes up for you in the moment. In a session, they can help you access the feelings still present from the past, the feelings you sometimes get triggered to, and they can help you return to the safety of the present moment. This person doesn't let you tell the same story in the same way because doing so can reinforce the trauma. They are intentionally intervening in your story to slow you down and to help you have new experiences of yourself as whole, safe, and capable of making good things happen.

They see the value of any resistance. They also make good use of the thoughts, feelings, and sensations you have when you relive positive moments, and they use these thoughts, felings, and sensations as medicine to help heal your wounds and difficult patterns.

In addition to psychotherapies, such as EMDR, EFT, somatic experiencing, and sensorimotor psychotherapy, I also recommend complementary therapies and activities that engage the body directly— such as: massage therapy, myofascial release, manual physical therapy, craniosacral therapy, pilates therapy, Feldenkrais Method, mindfulness, and yoga— with practitioners who are holistically oriented and professionally trained in their discipline.

We need different kinds of help at different times in life, and there are at least as many ways to heal as there are to be hurt. I encourage you to keep looking until you find what fits for you at each subtle bend and corkscrew turn along the path of your human development.

Summary

Inner dialogues that challenge generous giving:
1. I don't know what to do.
2. I know what to do, yet some part of me doesn't want to give to you generously right now.
3. (After lashing out or shutting down) I knew what to do. Why couldn't I do it?
4. Oh no, I messed up. Now it's too late.
5. I know what to do. I'm doing it, and it doesn't seem to be helping.

 In Which Direction Lies Your Growth?

- As you reflect on the challenges of generous giving, what was a time when your partner needed the Spotlight and you weren't able to give?
- Which challenging inner dialogue compels you most strongly when giving becomes difficult?
- When you come upon one of the challenges, how might you respond compassionately toward yourself?
- What new habits would you like to create?

*   *   *

IS IT OVER THERE?

CHAPTER 5

COURAGEOUS RECEIVING/REVEALING

———

"So, wait, you wanted me to come over, and now I want to come over, and you don't want me to anymore?"

"Right. Just forget it," she says.

"Can we do the Spotlight with this?" he asks.

"No." She pauses. "Okay, fine. We can."

"Okay, I'll be in the Giving role first," he says. "I'm really glad you're talking to me about this. What are you feeling?"

"I don't know. I'm annoyed. I'm angry."

"Angry, right. Of course you're angry—because the meaning you make is... what is the meaning you make?" His eyes are lovingly locked with hers.

"That you don't really want to come over."

"But I just said I wanted to."

"You're pulling the Spotlight back to yourself."

(Sigh) *She's right.* "Okay, let me try again. So, of course you're angry because the meaning you make is that I don't want to come over, and if I don't want to come over that means...?"

"I don't matter to you."

"'I don't matter to you' is the meaning you make. Oh, yeah, this must feel…" He pauses to sense what she's feeling. "This must feel awful."

"It's embarrassing," she whispers, hiding her face.

"Oh, embarrassing. I'm so glad you told me." He lowers his voice. "Do you know what you need for your embarrassment?"

"No. It makes me want to push you away and say I don't want anything at all."

This is more than she's ever revealed before, and he smiles at the trust building between them.

* * *

This conversation demonstrates intimacy. In the past, she's been overwhelmed by her feelings coming to the surface. Wanting and missing him can feel embarrassing to her because her needs for closeness haven't gone well in other relationships.

At face value, "I want to push you away" sounds like distancing yet means quite the opposite: She's connecting with him by revealing, and he's secure enough within himself to stay in the moment with her. They have also likely come to trust that they can give voice to different parts of themselves—like the part of her that wants to push him away and the part of her that doesn't—and they can each spend time in the Receiving/Revealing role.

Although easy to overlook, receiving is a vital element to the flow in your relationship, so let's make sure you're able to let all the good stuff in.

Spotlight Receiving Moves

When your partner is giving you loving care and attention, you are in the Receiving role. However, the question still remains: Are you actually receiving the love into yourself, into your heart and your being?

Your responsibility in the Receiving role is to check your internal "How-fully-am-I-receiving-right-now" gauge and communicate this reading to your partner. Speaking this Move aloud:

- Helps you remember receiving isn't passive. You are an active participant.
- Highlights the parts of you in need of love and compassion.
- Can help redirect your partner if their giving is not attuned to your needs in the moment.
- Is essential to your balancing as a couple.

Courageous receiving means allowing yourself, the real and evolving you, to be seen, known, and cared for as you reveal your innermost thoughts and feelings in an unguarded way. Why is this courageous? As much as we want to be known for our gifts, our struggles, and everything in-between, past experiences including rejection and neglect can increase self-protection. Some of this can be healthy. Guardedness has its place—as does courageous risk-taking in order to see what might be possible.

Spotlight Revealing Moves

Revealing Moves are intertwined both with the skill of receiving and with trust that your partner will be responsive to you from their Giving role. On one hand, it doesn't make sense to reveal yourself vulnerably if nobody is going to be there for you. On the other, how can you know what's possible until you risk revealing?

Does it matter *how* you reveal yourself? Yes, of course! According to Paul Weiss, an expert in Pragmatic/Experiential Therapy for Couples:

"One of the most important differences [between success and failure in intimate relationships] involves how people react when they feel upset."

Communication occurs with your AWE and myriad nonverbal cues. For Spotlight revealing, we will focus specifically on the three Moves below.

MOVE 1:
"I FEEL ____" (SAD, MAD, SCARED, ANXIOUS, FOGGY)

As you learn this Move, I encourage you to stick with a feeling you are having. We often say "I feel" and then talk about thoughts instead of feelings, which works just fine much of the time. When reaching for greater connection, however, actually feeling our feelings and communicating about them often helps.

For example, if you say, "I feel like you're really upset about your father," this is a *thought* you're having about the other person, whereas, "I feel anxious when you're on the phone with your father," is a statement about your own feelings.

Beginning with a feeling is revealing and a great help to your Giving partner, who is working hard to understand and empathize with your emotions.

Revealing thoughts and feelings doesn't mean you must share your deepest self all at once. It does mean you share something genuine for your partner to respond to, even if it's, "I don't know what I feel," or "I'm feeling this way *and* I don't know why."

When naming feelings and differentiating them from thoughts, the terms **sad**, **mad**, or **scared** cover a lot of emotional ground and tend to be easy to remember. I add in

anxious or **numb/foggy** because these are the experiences for many under stress about their primary relationship. **Embarrassment** is another important feeling that can require a little more unpacking because revealing embarrassment can bring up more embarrassment and even **shame**. Bringing these feelings into the loving care of your partner's attention allows you to attend to them together.

Joy and Celebration

In addition to how partners respond to the feelings described above, how they respond to each other's joy is vital. In fact, in their article "Will you be there for me when things go right?" Shelly L. Gable, Gian C. Gonzaga, and Amy Strachman found responsiveness (in the form of understanding, caring, and validation) to positive events to be more closely related to relational well-being than responsiveness to negative events.

Sometimes one partner's joy, passion, or celebration brings up insecurities or self-doubt in the other. If insecurities keep your partner from being able to give and join enthusiastically with you in your joy, then naturally you would be less inclined to reveal the good stuff. Additionally, if your joy wasn't validated in your family of origin, then perhaps you learned not to expect that your partner will celebrate your joys and successes along with you.

If your partner is having a hard time giving when you're experiencing joy, they may need time in the Spotlight first—to resolve their own inner conflict around this life-giving partner exchange. On the other hand, if your partner is your biggest fan and you are still having trouble revealing joy and receiving positive attention, the next chapter offers additional insights for easing into any vulnerability you might be feeling about your strengths, gifts, and joys.

What If You Don't Know What You Feel?

In this case, the Move is:

> "I want to know,
> *and*
> I want to tell you,
> *and*
> I just don't know yet."

Other candid answers include, "I don't know how I feel, *and* I don't want to find out!" or "I don't know, *and* part of me doesn't want to find out."

If you do know what you feel and you aren't quite sure your partner will be there for you, then it makes sense you might be hesitant. Just make sure you're checking to see if the story you're telling yourself about your partner's abilities is up to date.

Is your Giving partner present with you physically, emotionally, and energetically? If they are more present than before, can you risk revealing more than before?

One Bucket Is Plenty

Part of holding onto yourself in this Revealing role means keeping the focus on your own inner experience. Imagine you and your partner each have buckets in front of you for your feelings. One bucket for you, and one bucket for your partner. As you reveal yourself, stay with the feelings in *your* bucket. A frequently expressed concern is:

"I'm afraid my feelings will hurt my partner."

Even though you care about your partner, you are not responsible for the feelings in their bucket. If you bring up something that's important for you and your partner reacts by shining the Spotlight back on themself by saying something like, "I can't believe you said that!" or "It's so hurtful you feel that way," or "Why are you telling me this now?" they are simply showing you something in their bucket needs attention too. This isn't necessarily a problem.

If you're calm enough, you can remind them, "I care about what you're saying, *and* I'm trying to tell you something about me right now." If both of you have agreed to use the Spotlight, this is usually enough to get you back on track, where you can work together to decide whose bucket gets attention first. Keep in mind, the aim is to be *responsible for* yourself and *responsive to* your partner.

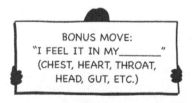

BONUS MOVE:
"I FEEL IT IN MY_____"
(CHEST, HEART, THROAT,
HEAD, GUT, ETC.)

Partners who are in touch with where they feel emotions in their bodies might reveal what they're experiencing in terms of physical sensations. Revealing sensations can help partners understand where emotions like sad, mad, and scared live in the body. Common expressions include a tight chest, racing heart, pit in the stomach, lump in the throat, or foggy feeling in the head. If you're interested in this bonus Move, I recommend letting this be an exercise of gentle noticing to see what arises for you.

As a willing partner, your intention in this Revealing role is to be felt and understood. Sharing sensations is yet another way to reveal yourself with clear signals and statements.

The Meaning You Are Making from Your Thoughts

Phrases such as "the meaning you make" help remind us that *we are creating meaning* from the thoughts and emotions flying through our bodies and minds. Reminding ourselves of other meanings we could possibly make is a useful exercise, as we can sometimes sort out our fears in the process. Once the fears and worries are conscious, we can examine them and bring care to the part of self that needs attention.

For most of our days, we're not even consciously aware we are having thoughts and beliefs about ourselves. Often it seems we go directly from what prompted us to what we said or did without noticing beliefs and emotions lie in between. Let's look at a few examples.

They're late

If my friend is late meeting me for coffee, my process can look like this: They are late, I lash out, I give them the cold shoulder, or I passive-aggressively show up even later the next time. When in fact, there are physiological reactions, feelings, and beliefs in between their lateness and my behavior, such as the fiery sensation in my belly, my feeling of anger, and my belief that I'm not very important to them. *Late* doesn't always equal *anger*, and we know this because not everyone would react the same way. Believing I'm not very important to my friend is the meaning I am making.

To some extent, we can choose our thoughts, but first we must become *aware* of them and resolve any emotional reactions that override the truth of our who we are. Once I know with my head, heart, and gut that I matter to my coffee date—and once I know I matter, period—then their lateness is not something I equate with my value.

I could also be someone who loves coffee shops and welcomes a few extra minutes to take in my surroundings so when my friend shows up late, I don't experience any negative reaction. Either way, the meaning making is happening inside *me*. My friend is the same number of minutes late in both situations.

They go silent

Let's consider a common belief with romantic partners: *When my partner doesn't say anything, it means they don't care about me.* This is meaning making. Your partner's unresponsiveness could have many other meanings.

For example, they could be feeling overwhelmed or physiologically flooded and unable to respond. This doesn't mean you're doing anything wrong by having feelings—or by failing to notice their distress. Flooding is sometimes only detectable with instruments that measure heart rate and breathing. Being flooded doesn't mean they're doing anything wrong either. If they are in the Revealing role, you will have the opportunity to attend to this gently. If they tend to become flooded in the Giving role, they will have to work on this reaction in order to be able to hold onto themselves while reaching for you.

An alternative meaning you could make would be, *When my partner doesn't say anything, this means they could be having a reaction right now.* It could also be true that your partner is having a reaction not because they don't care but because they care so much (i.e., you are very important to them, and something about this situation impacts them such that they have difficulty connecting in these moments).

They're trying to hurt me

When your partner speaks to you with an intensity that overwhelms you, you may think, *They are intentionally trying to hurt me.* This is also meaning making. What we often discover is that partners described as *intense* are coping with their fear of disconnection. Their strong expressions are usually an attempt to get you to engage because you are very important to them. An alternative meaning you could make in this situation is: *When my partner raises their intensity, it's not because they're trying to hurt me but because they're feeling scared right now.*

MOVE 2:
"I WONDER/WORRY
_____"
(ABOUT ME)

This Move includes your insecurities and your doubts about yourself. For example, "I wonder/worry that I'm _____" (i.e., too much, not enough, not important, or I can't make good things happen.)

Regardless of the origin, sometimes we develop inaccurate beliefs or illusions about ourselves that literally get tangled up with our physiology. One way to disrupt a negative cycle is by working hands-on with a client's physical and energetic body. To learn more about how a body-oriented therapist thinks about helping clients transform cycles and patterns, I interviewed Christopher Roberts, PT, IMT.C, a practitioner and expert in the field of manual physical therapy.

"Patterns of physical tension, thought processes, emotions, and energy affect us on a day-to-day and second-to-second basis as we integrate the world around us. These patterns are the screen through which we perceive, interpret, and react to our environment. Often a pattern plays out so quickly we're not even consciously aware it exists.

When a pattern is locked down, we react in a predetermined way because our systems are telling us it's about survival. In these moments, there is a confusion such that we aren't in present time and space, and we aren't aware we have options for responding differently.

Patients may conclude that the tension or anxiety is due solely to a present situation or that that is how they just are. They've learned to cope with an edgy or anxious feeling by limiting their lives. This means they might avoid certain places or situations they would otherwise enjoy because they are trying to manage the activation of their nervous system and the responses they receive from others."

Manual physical therapy addresses structures in the body, including fascia, bone, nerve, artery, vein, lymph, organ, skin, and muscle. Similar to the way in which some psychotherapies help clients create a pause so they can come back to the present moment and the truth of their experience, manual physical therapists help separate the tension in the physical tissue, which also creates a pause and the opportunity for the patient to experience themselves and others differently.

If you are drawn to modalities that address physiology directly, I encourage you to find a practitioner who can help unlock your body's inner wisdom, thereby giving you another pathway to consider as you decide what, when, and how to reveal yourself to your partner.

MOVE 3.
"I WONDER/WORRY
IF YOU _____"
(ABOUT ME)

This revealing Move is similar to the one above in that the focus is still on you, although this time you are explicitly revealing your worried guess of what your partner might be thinking.

For example, consider the statement, "I wonder if you think I'm too much of a problem and you won't want me anymore." This is vulnerable. As your partner in the Giving role becomes more and more skilled with this process, they will validate your feeling and reflect the meaning you are making first, rather than rushing in to fix it by saying, "Oh no, I never think that." While this statement might be reassuring at some point, most partners are most soothed by validation and reflection first, as these skills communicate empathy and understanding.

The toughest thoughts and feelings to reveal are often the ones closest to your heart, the ones you've protected because rejection in those areas is especially painful. Due to the tenderness of core thoughts and feelings and the likelihood that other thoughts, feelings, and defenses are layered on top, it's important to go slow.

Summary

Spotlight Receiving Moves:

- "I can receive this," or "I want to receive, and I can't right now."

Spotlight Revealing Moves:

- "I feel _____." (Examples: sad, mad, scared, anxious, foggy, etc.)
- "I feel it in my _____." (Examples: chest, heart, throat, head, gut, etc.)
- "I wonder/worry _____" (about me).
- "I wonder/worry if you _____" (about me).

 In Which Direction Lies Your Growth?

- Part of balancing is knowing when, what, and how much to reveal. Which is easier for you: giving or receiving/revealing?
- If in your Receiving/Revealing role you tend to reveal thoughts, could you focus on feelings? If you tend to be in

touch with feelings, would it help to notice the meaning you are making from your thoughts?

- Do you ever hold back on revealing joy?
- How can you expand your range of revealing on behalf of your relationship?

CHAPTER 6

CHALLENGES OF RECEIVING/REVEALING

————

Bring to mind a moment when you shared something in an unguarded way with your partner and then felt uncomfortable being the Receiver of the Spotlight. As you relive this moment as clearly as you can, see if any of these initial thoughts or challenges fit, even if you weren't aware of them at the time:

- Challenge 1: This attention feels so weird/uncomfortable that I don't even know what to do.
- Challenge 2: You're pitying me. I hate that.
- Challenge 3: I shouldn't have to tell you how I feel. You should know.
- Challenge 4: I'm so mad at you, I'm not giving you the satisfaction of helping me.
- Challenge 5: I've wanted this care and attention for so long, but now I just don't know.

Even if the moment that came to mind was quite a while ago, most of us can relate to one or more of these thoughts, and we can always benefit from learning to receive more deeply.

* * *

Receiving can be challenging because, even if you can clearly see your partner giving the care and attention you've longed for, some part of you might surface to deflect the kindness away. Let's explore what's happening in these moments.

Challenge 1: This Attention Feels So Weird/Uncomfortable That I Don't Even Know What to Do.

The intimacy of sustained eye contact alone prompts fidgeting, blushed cheeks, and many giggles between partners, so imagine what it might be like acclimating to a full range of attention, validation, curiosity, and support.

This challenge is often closely linked with underlying fears and blocks.As you read through the list of thoughts and fears below, pause to notice if any apply to parts of you that might resist receiving the Spotlight:

- Part of me doesn't believe deep down that I deserve care and attention. Am I even worth loving?
- Receiving from you is hard. Getting attention from people at work is easier. They are always happy with me!
- What's this all about? I don't need any attention.
- It's hard for me to take up space.
- When I really share what's inside, what if it's not enough for you? What if you find me boring or shallow?
- I don't know what I feel, and I know you want to know, and that feels like I'm disappointing you even more.
- If I let you focus on me, I get this feeling something bad will happen next.

Developing compassion for yourself in this way can take some time and exploration. Once you begin to honor the thoughts and feelings of different parts of you, then receiving your partner's care and attention becomes more familiar.

As an example of the last bullet point above, imagine a partner revealing that in childhood their parent would say, "Good job, you got an A!" followed by, "Now look at you: all proud of yourself. You must think you're so special," in a sarcastic tone. Maybe later in adulthood the same pattern continued with a partner who would say things to them like, "Hey, thanks for cleaning the garage. I never thought you'd get it together."

Understandably, when a positive reflection is repeatedly coupled with a negative, then receiving gets linked with negative expectation and risk. An honoring self-statement would be, "Of course I learned to deflect attention. It was always followed by sarcasm and criticism." With this, one validates their own experience, likely in the same way as their Giving partner.

Understanding how you learned to associate receiving attention with a negative outcome or feeling is critical. This association now exists inside of you, which is empowering news because once you become aware of it, you and your partner together have the loving power to rewrite those associations during your moments of receiving. Why *during?* When you're in a familiar bind with your partner, the old wound is exposed and opened enough to be cleaned out and cared for. To experience the same old feeling and have a new, positive emotional experience with your beloved person is what creates lasting change.

Other validating self-statements related to the list of fears could include:

- Of course I question whether I'm worth loving. I haven't felt very loved for much of my life.
- It's definitely easier to get attention from other people. Facing how much I want to be enough for you scares me.
- In many ways, I had to take care of myself from an early age, so it makes sense that I tell myself I don't need anything.
- Whenever I took up space or received attention at home, my parent looked at me disapprovingly. I'm afraid of shining too brightly.
- Yes, finally, it makes sense to me that I often don't know how I feel. My feelings were never that important to anyone, and I definitely didn't learn how to name or pay attention to them. They are even kind of embarrassing. This is all new to me.

From your Receiving/Revealing role, notice what you are thinking and feeling in the moment. You don't need to know more than you know right now. Tomorrow or next month you can reveal what you notice then. Partners are often comforted to discover how connected they feel when they slow down and learn to express what is current. Even to communicate genuinely in the moment, "I feel something, *and* I don't know what," carries an aliveness that allows for connection.

This is another good opportunity to practice adding the word *and* between statements that are true for you. For example:

It makes sense to me that I tell myself
I don't need anything,
and
I am learning that we all have needs.
I can reveal my needs to my partner as I notice them.

Challenge 2: You're Pitying Me. I Hate That.

While the expression of pity does typically include a type of compassion, it also comes laced with an air of superiority (i.e., *I pity you or your situation, which is different from—and inferior to—mine*), whereas Spotlight care recognizes we're in this together. We all have core emotions in need of attention.

If your partner is offering genuine and involved care and compassion from a mindset of *we*, but your brain has learned to associate any kind of care with pity, then you might understandably have the reaction of deflecting the care away.

Was there a time in your life when you learned to associate care with pity? A time when you might have decided on some level that having feelings makes you weak, or when you identified yourself as the one to give but not receive care?

Sometimes we build inner walls to guard against feelings, and there are instances when this ability is extremely useful. Think of caretaking and protective roles (e.g., a soldier, police officer, firefighter, EMT, surgeon, or caregiver of a sick family member), all of which require a shift of inner resources into action on behalf of the other, without any time to attend to one's own feelings. The challenge comes when we put up walls and can't take them down. For every role that asks of someone to *soldier up*, there also needs to be a time of *soldiering down*. An unguarded time when feelings and thoughts can be revealed and received.

Any shame around these human needs must be addressed in order for both partners to benefit from Spotlight giving and receiving.

Challenge 3: I Shouldn't Have to Tell You How I Feel. You Should Already Know.

Before you can receive loving care, you need to be able to reveal yourself—your thoughts, feelings, and inner experiences—as best you're able. Otherwise, how will your partner be able to respond to what matters most to you? As the writer Spuds Crawford says:

"If you expect me to read your mind you're going to have to think more clearly."

Being able to feel, identify, and reveal what's going on inside helps you bring your own awareness into being. Yet many partners can fall into the "You should know" trap, which is really more of a block. With this block, the belief is often: *I shouldn't have to say it. You should just know how I feel, what I think, or how hard this is for me.*

This belief or wish is understandable. For example, children develop healthfully when parents do anticipate and help them understand their needs at each stage. If a person didn't receive this nurturing in childhood, there could be some leftover longing that is indirectly placed on their partner. Even if one's childhood was warm and connected, there is a human longing to be known.

Having this longing is not shameful. As with any of these underlying beliefs, they make sense when we understand where they come from. Revealing this longing with your partner could sound like:

"I know it's not your job to predict my needs
or know what I'm feeling,
and
part of me really wishes you would!"

Saying this consciously rather than making an unconscious request to be rescued gives your partner the chance to validate all parts of you, which can be remarkably freeing and a good opportunity for playfulness and building trust with each other.

Popular culture supports the "You should know" trap by romanticizing the notion that relationships just happen and last without conscious attention. According to the premise of most movies, directly revealing your needs and actively receiving care shouldn't be necessary, yet in real life it is detrimental to the balancing of the relationship when a partner abdicates their healthy assertiveness.

Making the decision to reveal yourself to your partner as clearly as you can is necessary and empowering. Even if the signals you send are not yet clear, bringing yourself forward and earnestly expressing your intention for them to become clear is important. As the poet Mark Nepo writes:

> "Unconditional love is not so much about how we receive and endure each other, as it is about the deep vow to never, under any condition, stop bringing the flawed truth of who we are to each other."

This is the mindset shift from: "You should know without me telling you" to "I understand it's my responsibility to express myself."

Additionally, if your values include being the first line of support for each other, then there *are* times you can expect your partner to automatically show up for you. For instance, expecting your partner to be right by your side is reasonable: during times of loss, celebration, sickness, and extreme stress; if you're grieving or feverish; if your dog just died, your child has to go to the hospital, you graduated, received a promotion, or suffered a big disappointment. And when they are there, can you receive their care?

Interdependence means navigating life stronger together than apart. Willing partners know these big life moments are opportunities to show each other what loving is all about.

Challenge 4: I'm So Mad at You, I'm Not Giving You the Satisfaction of Helping Me.

You're feeling angry! Start by revealing this. If your Giving partner is learning how to hold onto themselves in order to keep the Spotlight on you, they'll be able to say, "Oh, you're mad at me. Tell me about this!" I know, it sounds superhuman, and with practice it does become regular human—that is to say, possible much of the time. Anger points to something important and finding out what that something is will be imperative to move through the conflict healthfully. We get confused when we think of anger as a behavior. Criticism, blame, stonewalling, and defensiveness are common behaviors associated with anger but are separate from anger as an emotion.

Dr. Bernard Golden writes about anger in his descriptively titled article, "How Disavowed Anger Contributes to Suffering: Anger that is denied doesn't go away. It demands our attention," saying:

Anger is a natural emotion, but we pay a huge price when we deny, minimize, or ignore it. By doing so we turn attention away from more fully recognizing our internal landscape. Through this process, we become less connected with ourselves—less aware of our desires, needs, and what moves us in general. Additionally, disavowal of such anger saps our energy and undermines our capacity to be empathic with our own suffering and that of others. It entails a denial of our humanity, thus making us less available to genuinely recognize the humanity of others.

Embracing anger as an emotion allows associated feelings of fear or sadness to surface, as well as the beliefs we have about ourselves not being enough or not mattering. If it feels right for you, consider asking yourself what feeling, deep care, or belief about yourself is being sheltered by your anger. If you are someone who claims to never feel anger, what would it be like to allow this part of you to receive validation, attention, and care?

Sometimes anger gives us the energy to be a little stronger and a little bolder about what we want. If you heal from past hurts, you won't have the power of the anger to help you insist on the change you need for yourself. Instead, you'll have the power of love for yourself that won't let you settle for anything less.

Challenge 5: I've Wanted This Care and Attention for So Long, but Now I Just Don't Know.

Often one partner will ask the other, "Why couldn't you do this for me when I asked? Why only now with this book, or now with this therapist? Wasn't I important enough for you to do it sooner? Why do you respect someone else but not me when I'm saying the same thing?"

It must be so frustrating and sad to have tried so many times, and these important feelings deserve care and attention. At the same time, just as a collection of experiences created these painful parts of your relationship, a new collection of experiences of receiving care and attention will be needed to create a new reality together. Every collection needs a first, and sometimes that's easier to bring about with a therapist who holds you both.

The next time you're in the Receiving role during a Spotlight moment, notice if your partner is giving care and attention in a way that feels good. If so, are you able to receive just this for right now? Opening yourself emotionally can be really hard if you're not sure the care will last. You've walled off any longings to protect from further pain. Recognizing and revealing these longings is what makes receiving so courageous.

Sometimes, as a form of distancing, partners talk *about* feelings rather than *feeling* and revealing them in the moment. This strategy takes them away from connection. Learning to allow yourself to feel in the moment rather than just reporting on the feeling can take time and requires trust, yet once you're *feeling* what you're revealing, your partner will have an easier time attuning to you.

What Might Make the Difference?

When you offer your concerns into the space of the relationship, we don't know what will happen next. Nurturing each other's willingness to wait and see, as you reveal what you know in the moment, sounds like this:

"I feel happy—and scared. I've wanted this,
and
it feels really good,
and
I don't know if I can trust it yet."

"I know you are doing so much for me right now.
I'm grateful,
and
I'm still feeling anxious about it."

According to Dr. John Gottman, who has been researching couples for decades, stable marriages have a five-to-one ratio of positivity. Using the word *and* allows for more positivity because you're not limited to comparative statements. You can reveal difficult emotions when you need to and reveal all your gratitude too.

*   *   *

Sometimes a change in life stages can bring about a shift in perception with regard to receiving, as in one woman's story shared below:

For many years, I looked for my husband to be someone different than he was. I mean, I don't know that
I consciously thought I would change him, but I
thought he would become an evolution of how people *should* be. When it didn't happen in terms of him
changing drastically, I got frustrated. But now I can
look at the qualities he does have and appreciate them
versus resenting them.

I've forgiven him for not offering the physical and
verbal affection I wanted. I thought he had an unwillingness and that, somehow, he was upset with me or
needed to distance himself from me. With the help
of counseling, I could empathize and see through his
eyes. Rather than a willingness or unwillingness, I
began to see giving affection as a capability or an inca-
pability. If you look at his history, he's not affectionate
with anyone. So I was expecting something of him
that was completely foreign.

Now that his work situation has changed and is
less stressful, we have a plethora of time to be together.
I've also been exploring why I depend on someone else
to make me happy. By taking responsibility for myself,
I was able to change the script about my husband and
what he brings to the table.

We're very comfortable in a desirable way. I think
the word *comfortable* is sometimes used to mean com-
placent, but this comfort feels safe. I grew up in a very
tumultuous household, so this kind of steadiness is
very calming for my nervous system and something
I now appreciate about him. I'm not saying it's one
hundred percent of the time. We're still a process and
an evolution.

Summary

When partners begin to understand the part of self that is brought to the forefront, then fears about receiving and revealing make so much sense!

Inner dialogues that challenge receiving/revealing:

1. This attention feels so weird/uncomfortable that I don't even know what to do.
2. You're pitying me. I hate that.
3. I shouldn't have to tell you how I feel. You should know.
4. I'm so mad at you, I'm not giving you the satisfaction of helping me.
5. I've wanted this care and attention for so long, but now I just don't know.

 In Which Direction Lies Your Growth?

- How easily do you receive?
- Which, if any, of the challenges feel true for you?
- What self-validating statements would you like to remember?
- As you reflect on the challenges of receiving and revealing, what healing are you drawn toward?

*   *   *

PART II

GOOD TO KNOW

CHAPTER 7

THE DRAMA TRIANGLE

Have you ever experienced the same frustrating, heart-breaking pattern in which, despite your best efforts, you keep getting sucked back into ways of relating that are either destructive or just don't feel good? If so, you might be on a drama triangle.

The Karpman Drama Triangle, created by Stephen Karpman in 1968 and adapted many times over, is a useful tool for understanding common negative patterns of relating. It helps explain why couples and families who aren't emotionally healthy nevertheless stay stable over time. Recognizing where you and your partner routinely get stuck and predictably switch roles on the triangle is an empowering first step toward greater health and happiness.

Three Roles and One Rule

The roles are:

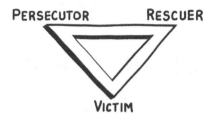

The rule is: If you play one role, you play them all. Even though you likely have one role where you spend most of your time, if you're on the triangle at all then you end up playing all the roles.

The following is a teaching story shared with me in 2008 by Cruger Johnson Phillips, former executive director of HopeWorks. The dialogue illustrates a drama triangle in action. Many who hear this story see parallels with regard to dynamics in their own relationships.

The Story of Sara and Walter

Years ago, my friend Sara calls me in the middle of the night and says, "Cheli, can we come over? Walter has been drinking again, and I'm scared."

I hear the fear in her voice, as I say, "Of course, come right over."

Let's pause our story here and notice the roles. Who is the **victim**? My friend Sara. Who is the **persecutor**? Walter, who has become frightening to Sara. And who dons her cape and acts as the **rescuer**? Me.

Sara comes over, and we stay up all night talking while her daughter sleeps in the next room. She decides that tomorrow morning she's going to move in with her sister. She's leaving Walter because he's not seeking help even though he feels badly about his behavior. She tells me they go through this every six months or so.

The next morning, I go into work, feeling good that I was there for my friend when she needed me. When I come home that night, however, I discover she's still in my house. Plates of partially eaten food litter the family room, and they must have returned to her house for toys, which are now strewn about.

"What happened? I thought you were going to your sister's?"

"Oh no," she says. "Walter called. We're going to talk about getting counseling. Everything will be fine."

If we pause our story here, what roles are we in?

Well, I've become the victim because I stayed up all night, my place is trashed, and nothing changed. Sara is now the one persecuting me, and Walter has come to her rescue with the vague offer of counseling.

Some time goes by, and I decide to call Sara, see how she is, and ask how counseling is going. We've been friends since second grade, and I don't want my frustration to keep us apart.

I call. "Hi, I miss you, and I've been thinking about you. How is counseling going?"

"Oh, we decided we don't need counseling. We need a bigger house. That's the problem. We're just too cramped here."

Before she has even finished her sentence, I lose it and start yelling, "Are you crazy? A bigger house? That's not going to help. Walter still hasn't dealt with his drinking problem. What's wrong with you two that you can't see that? This will just keep happening!"

Through the phone, I hear a sniffle that tells me her eyes are brimming with tears, as Sara says softly, "How could you say that about my Walter?"

Yes, Walter is now the victim. I have become the persecutor of Walter, and Sara comes to his rescue.

So, you see, if you play one role, you play them all—even if the roles flip quickly.

Do you recognize a drama triangle scenario playing out in your life? If so, you might be wondering, *How do I get off this crazy-making thing?*

Extricating Yourself from a Drama Triangle

Think of a drama triangle like a mobile hanging over a baby's crib. The pieces will shift and rotate, and they might bounce a little. Overall, the mobile itself stays steady. Drama triangle interactions stay steady too—until someone decides to change their role.

One approach to leaving a drama triangle involves getting to know different parts of yourself. According to transactional analysis, developed by Eric Berne in the late 1950s, we each, no matter our age, have three parts within us: a Parent, an Adult, and a Child. Additionally, the Parent is seen as two distinct parts: a Judgmental Parent and a Nurturing Parent.

Some aspects of these parts are as follows:

- The **Judgmental Parent** is critical and fault-finding. This part can, at times, be helpful (e.g., when teaching a child not to run out in the street).
- The **Nurturing Parent** is caring, loving, receptive, warm, and always there. This part can, at times, be overindulgent.
- The **Adult** speaks the facts even if the facts are about feelings and conveys said facts with little emotion.
- The **Child** is full of wonder, life, and energy. This part can also be rebellious and egocentric, as in, "I don't need you, and I'm not going to share!"

The theory goes that these parts of self relate to parts on the drama triangle. The Judgmental Parent is most like the persecutor.

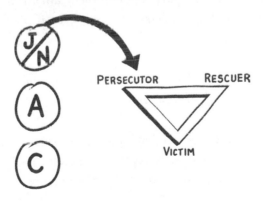

The Nurturing Parent is most like the rescuer.

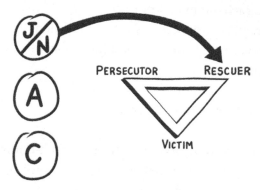

And the Child is most like the victim.

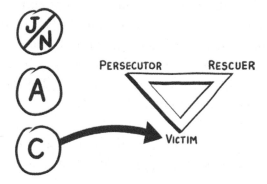

You might notice one part is not on the drama triangle: the Adult. The Adult part speaks the facts, even if the facts are about feelings.

> You exit the drama triangle by speaking and acting from the Adult part of yourself.

When Sara said they needed a bigger house, if I had been communicating love and acceptance for all the parts of both of us from my Adult self, I would have been more calm, open, soothing, and clear. I would not have said, "Are you crazy?" nor mocked their idea of a bigger house. I would not have said, "This is going to keep happening," because I don't know what will happen next.

Speaking from the Adult part of myself, I could have said:

"Sara, I'm so glad to know what's going on with you." (Spotlight Move 1.)

"A bigger house. You must be feeling so relieved to have a plan." (Spotlight Move 2, validating the feeling and reflecting her meaning.)

"*And* I'm concerned for you because there have been plans in the past, and it still doesn't sound like Walter admits he gets violent when he drinks. You said the pattern repeats every six months or so. I'm worried, *and* I respect that this is your journey."

We didn't do an official switching of Spotlight roles here, so I used the word *and* to add my thoughts and feelings without minimizing hers. In this statement, I was speaking from the Adult part of myself, expressing concerns without attempting to control her.

Sara might have still stated or implied that I was persecuting Walter; however, her implication would have been inaccurate since I was genuinely coming from the energy of the Adult part of myself.

If Sara was able to receive my giving when I said, "You must be so relieved, *and* I'm worried for you, *and* I respect that this is your journey," then I could ask her, "What do you need?" (Spotlight Move 3), while understanding I may or may not be able to give her what she requests. This will be something for me to discern when she makes the request. For example, if she asks, "Can you see how hard this is for me?" I could certainly offer extra validation: "Of course, it must be heartbreaking to have so much hope and be let down. It's also been about six months since the last time. That must be scary too."

If the cycle between them repeats and she expresses her need as a call to me at 2:00 a.m. to ask if she can come over, my challenge at that point will be to stay in the Adult part of myself during the crisis moment. This story is less about my answer and more about the part of myself from which I will engage in that conversation, the inner work I will need to do to stay in the Adult part, and the opportunities that might be created if I am able to do so.

Growing Pains: From Drama to Adult

The work we do in therapy includes:

- Working through emotional root causes;
- Transforming trauma into wisdom;
- Grieving what is lost; and
- Learning skills—such as validating feelings and needs— while challenging ineffective strategies.

This work enables one to stay in their Adult when conflict arises. As you may have already guessed, staying in your Adult during times of stress is also closely linked with the ability to be in the Giving role of the Spotlight.

Again, even if you do all the work and you stay in your Adult, you're going to be accused of being the persecutor at times because you might have information someone isn't ready for or doesn't want to hear. Often, the healthier you get, others who are still on the drama triangle will try pushing your buttons to get you back into your predictable roles and patterns.

Humans love familiarity, and your drama triangle companions need you to play your role to keep the thing going. This isn't from any malice or ill intent; things just work that way until awareness develops around these roles and motivations, inner experiences of reactivity are healed, and new skills are implemented.

Changes in important relationships can be painful. If you are faced with the choice of either staying on a drama triangle or setting boundaries to limit interactions with someone you love, I recommend finding trusted others to support you and provide an external reality check for how well you're staying in your Adult with your AWE.

Once you understand drama triangles, you'll see they can operate in any system: between partners, within oneself, in a family, an organization, or even among nations. No matter the reactions of others, when you exit the triangle, you model health and contribute to positive relational cycles.

Parts of Me, Parts of You

As mentioned earlier, we all have these parts (Judgmental Parent, Nurturing Parent, Adult, and Child) within us. Learning to identify the parts from which we are feeling, thinking, and behaving gives us a greater chance to make conscious choices about how we direct our energy and attention.

Although in real life the parts of us are fluid and changing in all our moments, I'm going to magnify aspects of the parts that contribute to drama triangle interactions.

Judgmental Parent

Let's say someone has:

 a very large Judgmental Parent part
 a small Adult part
 a small Child part

This person might often be critical and more likely to see shortcomings than gifts and strengths.

Nurturing Parent

Now, let's say someone has:

 an extra-large Nurturing Parent part
 a small Adult part
 a small Child part

This person might have a tough time setting boundaries and sticking with them.

Child

This person has:

 a small Parent part
 a small Adult part
 an enormous Child part

Although this person might be extraordinarily fun, they are also often not very reliable, helpful, or equal in adult partnership.

Adult

Lastly, this person has:

a small Parent part
a gargantuan Adult part
a small Child part

We can be tempted to think, *This is the best one!* and yes, during conflict and when you're trying to get off the drama triangle, communicating from your Adult part is best. Otherwise, though, too much Adult might be kind of—well—boring. The Adult speaks the facts but has a narrow range of emotion, after all.

We want to use the energy of all our parts well. By becoming as conscious as we can about which part we are experiencing and acting from, we can greatly improve the quality of our interactions and relationships.

Crossed Transactions

According to transactional analysis, crossed transactions (e.g., Adult-Parent, Adult-Child, Parent-Child) are created when one or both partners are acting unwittingly from non-Adult parts. These mismatched interactions can result in reactivity, disconnection, and ultimately resentment.

For example, one dating partner says to the other, "I notice you don't return my messages. Why is that?"

Their partner responds, from their wilting victim stance, "You're right. I'm no good. I don't even know why you're with me..."

The first partner then rescues by saying, "Of course you're good. I love you so much." Then, with more intensity, "What about the messages, though? Why are you dodging my question?"

To which the other, continuing the victim role, responds, "You don't have to be mean about it."

Being accused of meanness is the worst thing for the first partner to hear, so they then go into full rescue of self and partner by apologizing for their own frustrated feelings and dropping the topic all together.

In these crossed transactions, neither partner can stay in their Adult long enough to exit the triangle.

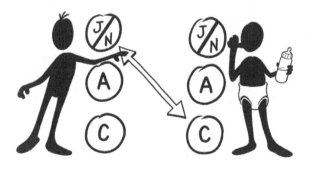

Resentments continue to grow until one or both parties leave the relationship or begin to own their drama triangle roles and make changes.

During conflict, any non-Adult part has the power to be just as unhelpful as any of the others. Nurturing and rescuing can sound more noble than Child and victim, but all non-Adult parts contribute to the cycle. Remember, if you play one, you end up playing them all.

Parallel Transactions

Parallel or complementary transactions (e.g., Parent-Parent, Adult-Adult, and Child-Child) flow easily, as each person feels heard and appreciated.

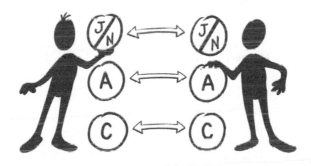

For example, if your Judgmental Parent is talking to your partner's Judgmental Parent, perhaps you balance that with the parallel transactions of your Nurturing Parent and Adult parts to create some firm and loving guidelines for your rambunctious pets.

If your Child self is playing with your partner's Child self, that's wonderful—how fun!

Likewise, if your Parent is consciously addressing your partner's Child, or your Child is consciously addressing your partner's Parent, these transactions can be instrumental to healing old wounds.

When conflict arises between the two of you, however, ultimately reaching parallel Adult-to-Adult states is an important way to create responsive partnership. The Spotlight Moves invite you to keep growing into your Adult self so you have the flexibility to call on that part as needed.

Summary

Recognizing when you're on a drama triangle can help you make sense of frustrating interactions that repeat. As a reminder:

- Drama triangle roles: persecutor, rescuer, and victim.
- Parts of self: Judgmental Parent, Nurturing Parent, Child, and Adult.

 In Which Direction Lies Your Growth?

- Do you recognize a drama triangle playing out in your relationship?
- If so, how do you participate? With which role are you most familiar?
- In what situations would you like to stay in the *Adult* part of yourself?
- What are some ways in which you and your partner enjoy parallel transactions?

CHAPTER 8

PURSUE-WITHDRAW

Demanding, criticizing, silent judging, stubborn heel digging—we've all dished out and received at least some of these less-than-kind behaviors, but what happens when partners repeatedly direct them at each other?

᛭   ᛭   ᛭

While we are complex and fully unique beings, we also operate in recognizable patterns that can help us understand ourselves. One of the most common negative patterns couples face is called **pursue-withdraw**. This pattern begins when one partner falls into the persistent role of **pursuing**, which often includes some form of demand, blame, or criticism, and one partner occupies the insistent role of **withdrawing**, which often includes some form of distancing or refusal to communicate.

Think of pursuit as turning up the heat or emotional intensity toward your partner and withdraw as turning the heat down, as if your relationship has a powerful dial that helps you regulate the intensity between you. The heat level rises and falls comfortably when you're securely connected. However, when you have a particular hot-button topic, or your relationship is in distress, insecurities and resentments can surface and it's easy to become overheated or overcooled in the process.

The Battle for Intensity

The couple pictured below is stuck in the pursue-withdraw cycle. They've fallen into this pattern so many times now that their roles are becoming entrenched with regard to this topic. Today, they are arguing about hugs.

Angry and sad about the amount of physical contact, the pursuing partner on the left reacts by turning the heat up and demanding attention. This is their way of saying, "I need you. Where are you?"

The withdrawing partner on the right feels worried by the uptick in emotion...

... and reacts by turning the heat down and dismissing the complaint, which is their way of saying, "When you're upset, I can't deal with the emotions I have inside."

The pursuing partner then concludes, "My feelings don't matter," which leads to more sadness and frustration. So they...

... double down on their original strategy even though it doesn't work: They turn the heat up even more, sure that if they can just get their partner's attention or explain themself well enough, then they'll be reconnected, which would be soothing to their nervous system. All of this makes sense on an individual level.

However, in the withdrawing partner's nervous system (which is quite possibly flooded and numbing out due to overwhelm), what makes sense is to...

... shut all this emotional stuff down. The withdrawing partner then doubles down on their original strategy, which is also ineffective for the relationship: turning the heat *off*, this time by going quiet and turning away.

The partner who wanted more connection ends up getting even less than before they asked, something which increases their feelings of frustration and loneliness.

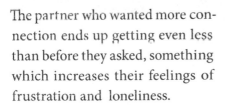

Both want a healthy and satisfying relationship. Sadly, the cycle leaves them feeling further apart.

While nuances exist, basic pursuing behavior often includes blaming, criticizing, raising a voice, overthinking, and insisting something be talked about, whereas withdrawing behavior often includes defending, going still and expressionless, avoiding the conversation through work or hobbies, trying to fix difficult feelings, or making a joke to divert attention.

What often can't be seen is that the pursuing partner is turning the heat up to restore connection and soothe their own anxiety, while the withdrawing partner is turning the heat down in an effort to protect the relationship and cope with their feelings, of which they are often unaware.

Of course, nobody is bad or wrong for feeling what they feel, *and* the impact of the behaviors on the other person can be immense. The withdrawing partner might describe themselves as being burned or cut by their partner's words, while the pursuing partner might say they feel starved or like they're bleeding out from the lack of connection.

Frustratingly, the more each partner tries to fix the problem according to what their sad, mad, scared, emotional brain is telling them is the best way, the worse the cycle gets and the more disconnected they become.

Each partner's behavior is understandable once we know what's happening for them on the inside. They are likely experiencing strong feelings and sensations or a lack thereof, plus thoughts and wonderings, such as:

- Why can't we just talk about it?
- Why can't this be easy?
- What happens if I upset you too many times?
- Do I matter to you?
- Am I ever enough?

- Am I too much?
- Can I count on you to be there for me?

Awareness of these underlying aspects can take some time to develop.

I'm Sorry, the Cycle Can Get Even Worse

As miserable as the cycle of pursue-withdraw is in the moment, its long-term impact can cause even more pain. In *Attached: The New Science of Adult Attachment and How It Can Help You Find—and Keep—Love*, authors Amir Levine and Rachel S. F. Heller note that with every negative encounter between an anxious pursuing and avoidant withdrawing partner, the anxious pursuing partner loses more ground. This helps explain a variation on the pursue-withdraw cycle in which the pursuing partner burns out or gives up on their efforts for greater connection.

When the pursuing partner becomes resigned to the current level of closeness that exists, the distance between the two often grows.

While pursue-withdraw is widely considered to be one of the most destructive patterns a couple will face, according to researchers and couples therapists Dr. Lynn Fainsilber Katz and Dr. John Gottman, the pattern also impacts future generations, as children of parents who exhibit this pattern experience greater anxiety, depression, and withdrawal.

In a synthesis of seventy-four studies on the pursue-with-draw pattern, the beginning of pursue-withdraw was found to be a signal the relationship may be deteriorating, thus highlighting the importance of addressing the cycle as soon as you become aware (Schrodt et al. 2014). Additionally, the longer the cycle lives in your relationship, the more difficult it is to change—and understandably so.

It can be hard to believe or allow yourself to care that your partner is actually feeling distress and missing the connection with you if all you see is intense pursuit or aloof retreat.

Both partners are speaking and acting from needs that are real and important, *and* they are often repeating strategies that simply don't work.

Behaviors or Entrenched Roles?

Before we explore possibilities for transforming these cycles or safeguarding your relationship from them, note that the behaviors of pursuing and withdrawing are different from the pursue-withdraw dynamic as entrenched roles in your relationship. We all resort to unhelpful pursuing or withdrawing. The danger begins when partners consistently dig in their heels with repeated behaviors due to repeated reactions, doing so without addressing underlying feelings and needs and without repairing the hurts that inevitably come as a result.

In a secure and balanced relationship, you notice these not-so-helpful behaviors in yourselves and point them out to each other. You say, "Ouch," figure out what's really going on, and repair things between you. In these instances, the moments of conflict and disconnection might be uncomfortable and frustrating, *and* you get through them without any lasting harm to your relationship. In fact, you get through them with greater confidence that you'll be there for each other the next time.

Pursue-withdraw as an entrenched cycle is different. When the behaviors described above turn into primary roles you play whenever you discuss that topic, then the cycle itself pits you against each other. You want so much to be on the same team and instead find yourselves feeling like you're on opposite sides. Rather than being a source of soothing, you become threats to the scared parts of each other. When that happens, your nervous systems can get overwhelmed. When you're caught in your cycle, time can feel short, options limited, and thinking becomes black or white rather than flexible. Your physiology changes as a result of the stress. On every level, you can lose your sense of togetherness when you need it most.

The Healing Power of Adult Relationships

Regardless of where you are on continuums of secure-insecure attachment and pursue-withdraw behavior and roles, we know adult romantic relationships have great influence over how we relate to ourselves and others. According to Levine and Heller:

"[Adult romantic relationships] are so powerful that they [can] actually revise our most basic beliefs and attitudes toward connectedness."

Primary adult relationships throughout our lives can bring out different aspects of our overall attachment styles, meaning parts of us are anxious and parts are avoidant. Parts of us pursue, and parts withdraw. When relationships are secure and balanced, these behaviors need not become entrenched roles.

The following is a story of contrasting experiences with pursuing, withdrawing, and security.

A woman I spoke with revealed that she had secretly thought of herself as a nagging wife because she pursued her husband in their marriage. She was usually the one to ask and often insist on more time and closeness. She spent time thinking about their relationship, coming up with new ideas to draw him closer, and she admits with regret that she often accused him of not caring about her.

Years following her divorce, she began to understand the avoidant part of herself when she dated someone who was more emotionally pursuing than she was. While dating one of these men, for example, she felt a stunned confusion come over her when he anxiously pursued her for more time together. She thought things were great between them, so these requests surprised her and felt like pressure. In time, she noticed she avoided the conversation whenever he anxiously asked about her availability. She was also hesitant to share other concerns she had. As the withdrawing partner in this relationship, she had now been on both sides of the pursue-withdraw cycle.

Owning her avoidant moves with her dating partner as well as her pursuing moves with her former husband gave her perspective and empathy. Years later, she found someone with whom she now enjoys a secure connection, one where she says they each have anxious moments and avoidant moments. In those times, though, they share their insecurities and reassure each other, and she's amazed that their momentary frustrations are just that.

Preventing or Transforming the Monstrous Cycle

As we explored previously, levels of pursuit and withdraw range from the occasional behavior to an entrenched cycle. If you're reading this book to proactively create a healthy foundation for your new relationship, the Moves offer direction to help you establish and maintain a balance of giving and receiving.

If you've been in a negative cycle of pursue-withdraw for some time, the Spotlight is a helpful tool to assess where you're stuck and coach you to new skills for partnership. You might find the process brings more joy and less suffering as you move toward balance and clarity. If this isn't the case and you're still experiencing the cycle as a monster pitting you against each other, it's important to find a professional who works with these cycles. Once they are entrenched, making changes can be very difficult without professional help.

For that help, I recommend EFT for couples, augmented with trauma therapies such as EMDR if either or both of you are experiencing reactivity that isn't improving markedly through the course of your therapy. By reactivity, I mean the aspects mentioned above (time can feel short; options limited; and thinking becomes black and white rather than flexible), as well as an awareness that you're anxiously turning up the heat—or shutting it down. If these types of reactions are becoming less frequent, less intense, and reducing in duration, this is a positive sign. I recommend keeping a journal so you can accurately assess your progress toward getting what you want for yourself.

Willing partners are curious to become more aware of their own inner world and to learn how their behavior impacts their partner's inner world. They care greatly about changing their own reactive patterns.

The Spotlight Moves help you regulate the heat on your relational burners.

Attachment Style

For decades, the field of psychology's leading explanation for whether a person tends to be more pursuing or more withdrawing overall is based on attachment style. Back in 1958, famous child psychologists John Bowlby and Mary Ainsworth identified how children bond with their parents and how they cope when separated from their parents. Bowlby and Ainsworth's work was revolutionary because it helped describe the difficult behaviors a child experiences during separation. The study of adult attachment recognizes the same three types of behavior experienced within an adult's primary relationship. Briefly defined, they are:

Secure: Securely attached people feel comfortable with the closeness of the relationship and confident in their partner's love for them.

Anxious: Anxiously attached people crave closeness, become preoccupied with the relationship, and are sensitive to any signs that their partner might not return their love. Their attachment systems—that is, the way they bond and cope with disconnection—have learned to turn up the heat when in distress.

Avoidant: Closeness and intimacy are uncomfortable for avoidantly attached people who value their independence over relationship. Their attachment systems have learned to turn off when in distress.

While pursuing is linked to an anxious attachment style and withdrawing to an avoidant attachment style, research continues to expand our understanding of what causes a particular kind of coping when our nervous systems are activated.

Summary

- Pursuing behavior includes blaming, criticizing, raising a voice, overthinking, and insisting something be talked about.
- Withdrawing behavior includes defending, going still and expressionless, avoiding the conversation through work or hobbies, trying to fix difficult feelings, or making a joke to divert attention.
- Pursue-withdraw patterns are serious and can quickly become worse. Every move you make to address underlying concerns and act on behalf of your relationship will help you regulate the heat on your relational burners.

In Which Direction Lies Your Growth?

- When do you turn up the heat in your relationship?
- When do you turn down the heat in your relationship?
- What are you thinking and feeling in these moments?
- What is the impact on your partner when you turn the dial? Think not only of what you see with your eyes but also imagine the thoughts and feelings your partner might be having. Could their heart rate be so high and their blood oxygen so low that they aren't able to hold onto themselves or reach for you in these moments?
- What is the impact of your partner's pursuit or withdraw on you?

PART III

GETTING CLEAR

———

CHAPTER 9

CLARITY
(AN ASSESSMENT)

───

This chapter is designed to help you assess and reflect upon your journey with the Spotlight Moves, the drama triangle, and the pursue-withdraw cycle. I encourage you (individually or as a couple) to return to the questions below as you continue to practice and learn.

Positive Memories

Sometimes while focusing on how to be closer, we can overlook positive shifts already made. Vividly reliving positive memories often reactivates the same feel-good thoughts, feelings, and physiological responses we felt at the time, which is beneficial for the moment and also helps partners become familiar with the feeling state they would like to inhabit more often.

The more time you spend in a particular emotional state, the more likely that state will become an enduring characteristic (a trait), hence the phrase coined by Bruce Perry, MD:

"States become traits."

<u>Exercise:</u>
Allow a positive moment of connection from any time in your relationship to come into your mind. Relive that one moment clearly with all your senses, including what you see and hear, the lighting and sounds, and your posture and proximity to each other in that moment. Zoom in on the best part of that one memory and let the good feelings get as strong as they want.

Then, if you're reading together as a couple, check in to see if you'd like to share your memories with each other. Do so as long as sharing is enhancing the positive.

Spotlight Assessment

As you are reviewing the assessment questions, I invite you to proceed with the mindset that adding even one new element to your awareness or skill set is cause for celebration. Every gesture matters, and even a seemingly small shift can create positive momentum.

Charts are available in the next section, both as an alternative to the questions if you prefer visuals and as a way to help pinpoint what Move needs attention if you're feeling stuck.

From the Spotlight Giving Role

1. When did I gratefully invite my partner into the Spotlight with "I'm so glad you told me!" or a similar phrase? Did my energy match my words? Does my partner agree?
2. When did I validate my partner's feelings with, "Of course you feel," or a similar phrase? Did my energy match my words? Does my partner agree?
3. When was I able to make the Bonus Move of reflecting the meaning they were making? Does my partner agree?
4. When was I able to help my partner choose from their menu of options by asking, "What do you need?" Does my partner agree?
5. When did I remember to ask, "Is there anything else about this?" Did my energy match my words? Does my partner agree?
6. When was I able to initiate the Spotlight shift to my partner?
7. When was I able to initiate the Spotlight shift to myself?
8. When did I circle back once I realized I missed something?
9. What am I still learning about myself in this role?

For a variation on the questions in this section, allow a memory of a time you were in the Giving role to come into your mind. If you see many moments, choose the one that stands out the most. Relive that one moment as clearly as you can, then answer the questions above based only on that one moment. Skip over the word *when* in each question for this variation.

From the Spotlight Receiving/Revealing Role

Receiving:

1. When was I able to receive my partner's loving care and attention? Did I let my partner know I could receive at that time?
2. If I wasn't able to receive, did I let my partner know, "I want to receive, *and* I can't right now," or not?
3. What am I learning about myself as the one receiving care and attention?

For a variation on the questions in this section, allow a memory of a time you were in the Receiving role to come into your mind. If you see many moments, choose the one that stands out the most. Relive that one moment as clearly as you can, then answer the questions above based only on that one moment. Skip over the word *when* for this variation.

Revealing:

1. When was I able to reveal some of my vulnerable feelings in an unguarded way with phrases such as, "I feel _____ (sad, mad, scared, anxious, numb/foggy)," or something similar?
2. When do I still blame, criticize, stonewall, or shut down? What helps me hang onto myself in these moments so I can reveal my thoughts and feelings vulnerably?
3. When was I able to make the Bonus Move of noticing where I felt my emotions in my body?
4. When was I able to share, "I wonder/worry _____ (about me)?"

5. When was I able to share, "I wonder/worry if you _____ about me?"
6. Am I able to stay focused on the current event? Or do I tend to bring in past moments?
7. What am I learning about myself as the one revealing my feelings and thoughts?

For a variation on the questions in this section, allow a memory of a time you were in the Revealing role to come into your mind. If you see many moments, choose the one that stands out the most. Relive that one moment as clearly as you can, then answer the questions above based only on that one moment. Skip over the word *when* for this variation.

Pause and Play

1. When was I able to pause? What makes pausing easier for me?
2. When did I remember to use the word *and* instead of *but* to hold multiple thoughts or feelings side by side? How did that go?
3. Did I find opportunities for play? Did my partner respond positively to my attempt at playfulness?

Bonus

1. When have I suggested to my partner that we use the Spotlight?
2. When have I asked to be in the Receiving role?

3. When have I offered to be in the Giving role first? How did it go?
4. How and how well do I help triage which of us receives the Spotlight first?
5. What am I still learning?

Spotlight Assessment (Charts)

Before beginning with the charts below, identify your role and the one Spotlight exchange you will remain focused on as you progress from one chart to the next. When you change your role or have a new Spotlight moment to assess, begin again with the first chart.

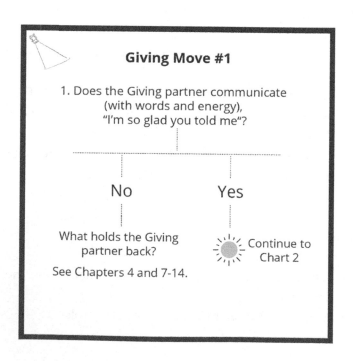

Giving Move #1

1. Does the Giving partner communicate (with words and energy), "I'm so glad you told me"?

No

What holds the Giving partner back?

See Chapters 4 and 7-14.

Yes

Continue to Chart 2

Receiving Move

2. Is the Receiving partner able to receive the welcome and invitation?

No

What is causing the deflection of this care and attention?

See Chapters 5, 6, and 7-14.

Yes

Continue to Chart 3

Giving Move #2

3. Does the Giving partner validate the feeling (with words and energy), "Of course, that must feel ____." Do they pause and proceed gently, "Is that it?"

No

Is there an emotional block or the need to practice this new skill?

See Chapters 4 and 7-14.

Yes

Continue to Chart 4

Receiving Move

4. Is the Receiving partner able to receive the validation?

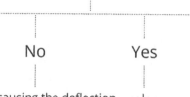

No   Yes

What is causing the deflection of this care and attention?

 Continue to Chart 5

See Chapters 5, 6, and 7-14.

Giving Move Bonus

5. Does the Giving partner reflect the meaning accurately enough? "The meaning you make is ____." Do they pause and gently confirm, "Is that it?"

No   Yes

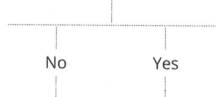

Is the Giving partner becoming stressed, activated, or overwhelmed? Consider switching roles briefly to reassure the Giving partner.

Continue to Chart 6

See Chapters 4 and 7-14.

Receiving Move

6. Is the Receiving partner able to receive the reflection?

No

Yes

What is causing the deflection? Perhaps a fear or an undercurrent?

See Chapters 5, 6, and 7-14.

Continue to Chart 7

Giving Move #3

7. Does the Giving partner ask, "What do you need?" and offer some of their partner's favorite menu items (e.g., a hug, more validation, problem-solving, "grrrr" together, etc.)?

No

Yes

Is the Giving partner becoming stressed, activated, or overwhelmed? Consider switching roles briefly to reassure the Giving partner.

See Chapters 4 and 7-14.

Continue to Chart 8

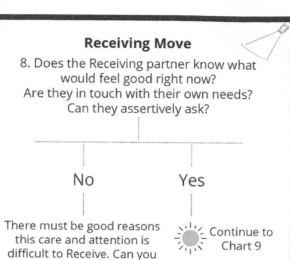

Receiving Move

8. Does the Receiving partner know what
would feel good right now?
Are they in touch with their own needs?
Can they assertively ask?

No

Yes

There must be good reasons
this care and attention is
difficult to Receive. Can you
be curious about the reasons
together?

Continue to
Chart 9

See Chapters 5, 6, and 7-14.

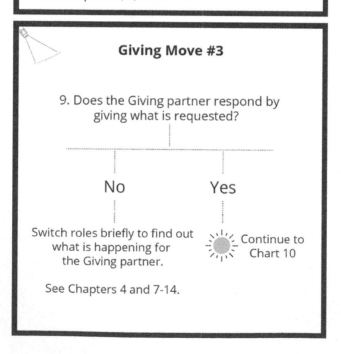

Giving Move #3

9. Does the Giving partner respond by
giving what is requested?

No

Yes

Switch roles briefly to find out
what is happening for
the Giving partner.

Continue to
Chart 10

See Chapters 4 and 7-14.

Receiving Move

10. Is the Receiving partner able to receive the care and attention being given?

No   Yes

Could there be a fear or an undercurrent? Is there something else about this topic?

 Continue to Chart 11

See Chapters 5, 6, and 7-14.

Giving Move #4

11. Does the Giving partner ask, "Is there anything else?" and find another time to discuss if needed?

No   Yes

Sometimes an agreed-upon break is helpful if there is more to discuss.

Begin the process again. Once resolved, continue to Chart 12.

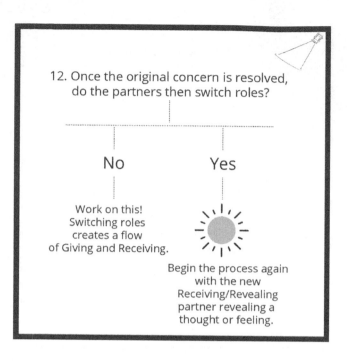

12. Once the original concern is resolved, do the partners then switch roles?

No

Work on this!
Switching roles
creates a flow
of Giving and Receiving.

Yes

Begin the process again
with the new
Receiving/Revealing
partner revealing a
thought or feeling.

Drama Triangle Assessment

1. When recently have I played the role of persecutor with my partner?
2. When recently have I played the role of rescuer with my partner?
3. When recently have I played the role of victim with my partner?
4. How did I get back into the Adult part of myself?
5. Did my partner see me as speaking from the Adult part of myself or acting as the persecutor or rescuer?
6. Were we able to use the Spotlight regarding these concerns?

7. What am I still learning about drama triangles, how I participate in them, and how to exit them?

Pursue-Withdraw Assessment

1. What pursuing behaviors have I exhibited recently?
2. What withdrawing behaviors have I exhibited recently?
3. Did the Spotlight help us get out of our negative cycle? If so, how?
4. Am I partnering as well as I would like in the areas my partner tends to advocate for?
5. Am I partnering as well as I would like in the areas I tend to advocate for?
6. What am I still learning about the pursue-withdraw pattern?

Positive Cycles

1. When did I notice my Moves having a positive impact on my partner?
2. When did I notice their Moves having a positive impact on me?
3. What was the impact? What did it feel like?
4. When did I use the word *and* to hold competing ideas side by side?
5. What is the ratio of my positive to negative comments toward my partner?
6. What am I still learning about creating positive cycles?

The above questions are designed to give you a sense of how your experience is affecting your relationship and what might still need attention. As you consider the questions, I encourage you to continue celebrating your progress and proceeding with gentleness toward yourself and your partner.

"Remember, we all stumble, every one
of us. That's why it's a comfort to
go hand in hand."

—EMILY KIMBROUGH

How We Impact Each Other

Balancing the energy of giving and receiving often leads to greater peace and fulfillment. If we look at a collection of the most joyful and most painful moments partners recall with each other, we hear the impact of the words we do and don't speak and the actions we do and don't take.

As unique as we are, we have similar wants and needs regarding consistent emotional responsiveness. When we see our similarities at core levels, then reaching for each other becomes more approachable.

*　　*　　*

"Oh, you get scared?"
"I do."
"Angry? Sad?"

"Yes, both."

"You feel it in your chest?"

"Yeah, sometimes, but mostly pressure in my head. What scares you?"

"I've been afraid of losing you, of being too much. I thought you couldn't possibly care. Now, I know you care so much about how we are together. I didn't know."

"And I've been afraid of losing you, of not being enough. I thought you couldn't possibly want the real me. Now, I'm getting it, and I want to be closer."

* * *

The intentional slowing and relaxing of your heart, your body, and your mind as you receive your partner's care, paired with the experience of yourself as someone capable of giving that care in return, creates new pathways of responsiveness and balanced relating.

* * *

CHAPTER 10

CYCLE MEETS CONTENT

———

"I'm lonely. You're not available anymore, so of course I want my family around."

"Not available? That's because I'm working all the time. In your eyes all I've ever been good for is money. Isn't that right?"

"No, that's not right. That's your story. Not mine."

In this exchange, partners say more than we think. They allude to loneliness, availability, family, money, worth, reactivity, and differing views. These short lines above are packed with emotion and meaning.

*   *   *

As a couple, you will explore and encounter many topics, values, events, and specific decisions. We can think of these different areas as the **content** of your relationship and interactions, while the cycles we have explored represent the **process**. We've spent a lot of time on process and emotional cycles—creating positive ones and learning how to identify tricky negative ones—precisely because responsiveness to each other's emotions is the most vital element of loving relationships.

"The greatest gift a parent has to give a child—and a lover has to give a lover—is emotionally attuned attention and timely responsiveness."

—DR. SUE JOHNSON

And, content matters too. Content areas such as parenting, finances, physical affection, sexual life, division of labor, and how you spend your leisure time will be uniquely yours and ever evolving. While the first parts of this book focus on skills and cycles, the remainder will provide additional considerations for clarity and understanding the goodness of fit in your relationship.

Meaning Making (Revisited)

As the cycles of our relationships turn, we create meaning about what is happening with regard to external events, our inner lives, and everything else! We form understandings and opinions. We generate stories, also called narratives, and make decisions based on these stories both consciously and unconsciously, both separately and together.

The principles of narrative therapy as developed by Michael White offer helpful suggestions for partners, including:

1. Seek to collaboratively expand the view of your relationship by including additional stories and meanings. (E.g., "I appreciate how you take care of us financially, *and* I'm taking care of us in ways that matter, too, such as _____ . How can we support each other?")

2. Address grand narratives which often contain hidden cultural "shoulds." For example, the appointed income earner in the family might believe they should also carry the emotional burden of that role alone. (E.g., "In order to be strong, I don't share my stress openly with my partner. I hold it all by myself.")

3. Emphasize the problem as the problem rather than the person as the problem. (E.g., "We want to spend more time together, *and* we have bills to pay," approached as, "We're on the same side of the table, and the problem is there, across from us.")

4. Ask yourself how you were recruited by a cultural story into particular ways of behaving that might not be a good fit for your core self and relationship. For example, if the cultural story is: *We have to stay stoic and independent in our separate responsibilities,* then exploring where and how you were encouraged to make this story your own can help you decide if it's one you'd like to keep or revise.

(Gallant 2011)

Sometimes our stories are clear to us, sometimes with a little guidance they become clear, and sometimes they are just plain confusing and take a while to sort out.

When couples are stuck in a negative emotional cycle, is the resulting debris creating their conflicting narratives? Or are their conflicting narratives jamming the gears of their emotional cycle?

Before we dive into the murky waters of these particular confusions, let's first take a look at more straightforward outcomes of cycle/content combinations.

Cycle and Content Interact

Couple 1: The Glow of "We"

If you have a mutually positive, emotionally responsive cycle overall, you can add many types of content with good outcomes. Positivity creates greater trust and more positivity!

You can see the emotional cycles for this couple's content areas are spinning in the positive direction. They invite and validate each other's feelings. They listen for and reflect the meaning and respond to each other's in-the-moment needs. When faced with new topics, events, or decisions, they have a baseline of confidence that they will find a way to work together as a loving team.

Couple 2: Vulnerable Revealing Makes All the Difference

Consider a common narrative a partner will reveal in therapy: "We just can't communicate." If both partners agree, then that's also their shared narrative: "We just can't communicate."

If one says, "We just can't communicate," and the other says, "No, that's not it. We're just too different," then they have different narratives about what's happening. Both of these are broad summary statements. With care and attention, we find out what the terms *communicate* and *so different* mean to each of them.

Even if one is saying, "We just can't communicate," and the other, "We're just too different," when we slow things down, we might discover they are actually talking about the same missing element. Maybe they both want to feel more appreciated and conclude they are not because they haven't heard the thoughts and felt the feelings beneath their outward behaviors.

When they hear how they are each protesting the disconnection in their own way and that they are doing so because they matter so much to each other, they are then more likely to lower their defenses and come closer once again. Language such as *we* and *our* often comes back online as their separate narratives transform into a shared one:

Our automatic pilot ways still kick in, but now we can give each other *the look*. Remember we told you about that funny look from the time we went to Cancún? Anyway, that look brings us back, and we remember to appreciate each other out loud again.

Because they had a mutually responsive cycle in other areas of life, vulnerable revealing wasn't new to them. They knew how to let down their guard about their feelings and thoughts. This enabled them to transform their story from one of separation to one of togetherness. From me-versus-you to *we*.

Couple 3: Complementary Content

Long-standing disagreements about content areas happen as well. These are the topics about which couples shrug and say, "Oh well, we disagree," without emotional distress. For example, maybe politically, one leans left and the other right. They can disagree about the issue while still recognizing that, at the most basic level, their priorities of valuing family time, being of service, and creating fun memories are nearly identical.

Their emotional cycle remains positive and responsive, and the narrative about their political differences then tells the story of what a great complement they are to each other, as they both value the deep thinking and intellectual intimacy that can come with respectfully debating opposing points of view.

Couple 4: New Discoveries That Can't Be Resolved at This Particular Time

Sometimes one partner discovers something new about themselves or their significant other, or a particular value or preference resurfaces and becomes more of a priority at this stage of life. For example, one partner decides they want to have children, when previously they didn't think they would. Their partner still isn't interested in raising a child. This couple has an overall positive emotional cycle *and* a content area they aren't able to resolve at this particular time.

While potentially sad, this difference is also clear and straightforward for them. They don't have the frustrating confusion of wondering, "What happened to us?" layered on top of any loss, and they have a better chance of cocreating a shared narrative that includes empathy for one another. Something like, "It just turned out that this important decision changed for us. We couldn't have known."

One might say, "I feel how much you want to become a parent, and I don't blame you. You didn't know until you knew."

Then their partner might respond, "And I don't blame you either. Something big shifted for me and not for you."

With this kind of dialogue, they can grieve and move forward healthfully.

Of course, couples also work through content issues previously considered *unresolvable* and are able to continue forward as a couple. We don't know how, when, or if an aspect will shift. The question these couples face is how long to stay in the process.

Couple 5: Entering the Murky Confusion

Now, let's consider partners who are caught in a negative cycle such that their disagreements on several hot-button topics are rarely resolved. Due to the layering of their negative cycles, resentments have been building. Lately, one feels frustrated and alone whenever they try to discuss sexual connection and how they handle money, and the other feels frustrated and alone whenever they try to discuss nonsexual physical affection and time with extended family.

Their behaviors of pursue and withdraw intensify as each pursues the other for the topic they care most about. Their inner emotional experiences are changing too. Where one used to feel anxious, they now notice they are numbing out. Where the other used to be somewhat unaware of feelings, they now feel anxious at the shifting sands in the relationship.

If this couple is faced with an additional stressor, such as the possibility of having a family member move into their already-cramped house, they will be a lot less likely to connect emotionally and create shared narratives about the new development. Their negative cycles regarding each topic have already blended into each other: financial choices, sexual connection, nonsexual physical affection, family time, and now Uncle Bert wants to move in for a while.

Blended cycles are complicated. Although this couple starts talking about Uncle Bert as the problem, along the way we find out:

The partner who is usually pursuing for affection and emotional connection begins to give up. Nothing seems to work, so they somewhat unconsciously begin spending more money and committing to more time with extended family.

It comes as a surprise to this partner that their own inner longing to be close seems absent. Something has shut this off, and this partner's behavior starts to look more withdrawing.

The partner who pursues for adherence to a budget feels betrayed and anxious with the increase in spending. This partner usually pursues for sexual connection, too, but lately even that is changing.

Noticing their partner doesn't even try to talk or ask for affection anymore, this partner starts to worry that maybe this situation is serious, and they could actually lose each other. Gathering up their courage to try reconnecting, this partner reaches out—just as Uncle Bert walks through the front door.

A week later the couple walks through my door arguing about Uncle Bert.

As you can see, this is difficult to sort out. As long as a negative emotional cycle exists, having productive conversations about priorities, agreements, and decisions (a.k.a. the content) is tough. Conversely, perhaps the emotional cycle is difficult to de-escalate precisely because there is underlying content that isn't yet conscious or spoken about.

Confusion about priorities, agreements, and decisions contributes to heightened emotions, and heightened emotions contribute to content confusions.

Positive new cycles are difficult to create when you're pulling a baggage cart full of hurts from the past. If your cart is full, I strongly recommend therapies designed to work through past hurts that prevent you from adopting new strategies.

As a therapist trained in both Emotionally Focused Therapies (EFT) for couples and Eye Movement Desensitization and Reprocessing (EMDR) for the treatment of trauma and stressful events, I concur with the benefits of integrating these two therapies, as outlined in a 2022 article featured in the *Journal of Marital and Family Therapy*, in which clients developed increased intimacy, self-regulation of emotion, and greater insight into their behaviors after simultaneous treatment. EMDR provides a productive avenue for accessing the root causes of the negative cycle, and EFT facilitates de-escalation and restoration of a couple's bond. Both work toward the goal of creating secure attachment and connection.

Hidden Content

If you have good help and your relationship still isn't thriving, perhaps this is due to a deep underlying content area or undercurrent that's difficult to see. These areas might be agreements you signed up for early in the relationship without realizing or expectations that have come about since that aren't a good fit for you now. Undercurrents could include secrets or profound changes that need to be discussed and consciously renegotiated before a positive responsive cycle can begin to form.

Summary

Emotionally responsive cycles help us navigate life's most difficult content, and major differences about content can make a responsive cycle feel impossible to establish. Let's proceed, exploring both cycle and content.

 In Which Direction Lies Your Growth?

- Do any of the couple scenarios above feel similar to yours?
- Do you have content areas that spin in a negative direction?
- Which content areas are the most positive and sustaining for you in your relationship?
- Are there any hurts in your baggage cart? What intentions or healing are you drawn toward?

CHAPTER 11

UNDERCURRENTS

"Here, let me help you. I know just what you need."
—FOUNDING MEMBER, OVERFUNCTIONERS ANONYMOUS

*   *   *

Undercurrents are the agreements, assumptions, or expectations that circulate out of view for one or both parties. They
can vary in their depth, level of strength, and proximity

to the foundation couples seek to build or rebuild. They almost always create some level of confusion until they are made conscious.

While these undercurrents do not represent an all-inclusive list, they are worth considering if the Spotlight Moves have not yet brought clarity and reconnection to your relationship.

Undercurrent: Fairness and Functioning

In their distress, a partner will often look to their therapist to help them resolve a question of fairness. Perceptions of fairness can be closely related to a partner's overfunctioning or underfunctioning within the relationship. These terms were coined by Murray Bowen, a family systems theorist who identified how these roles work in a cycle (similar to pursue-withdraw) in which as one partner overfunctions, the other underfunctions, and as one underfunctions, the other overfunctions. The functioning can be related to tasks or emotions (Bowen 1993).

Think of a middle stream where you as partners can enter together healthfully. Holding onto yourself means you are comfortable on your shore as an individual *and* comfortable reaching for your partner by wading into the stream together. This is the joy of secure relating.

Overfunctioning means you're on your partner's shore all the time, bringing along the excessive sunscreen and managing them due to your own fear or anxiety. If you are overfunctioning, I encourage you to come back to the middle and go no further. You lose connection with your own shore

if you go all the way over there, and your partner doesn't have the opportunity to experience missing you if you constantly overstep.

Underfunctioning means you retreat from the middle stream of partnership. Withdrawal holds tremendous power, although it's not the collaborative kind that helps you be better together. Underfunctioning often means walling yourself off and leaving your partner to carry everything alone. This may seem like a good strategy to prevent hurt, but at what cost? Walls also prevent trust and true connection.

Overfunctioning and underfunctioning dynamics thrive in drama triangles and cycles of pursue-withdraw. In contrast, a balance of giving and receiving/revealing creates streams that release you both to the world with each other's support and encouragement, and then pull you back in for reunion where you can share, recharge, and create once again. If the overfunctioning and underfunctioning behaviors don't subside altogether with well-functioning Spotlight Moves, at least the remaining tendencies are highlighted and brought to consciousness where they can be skillfully addressed.

The Challenges of Stepping In

There are many partners who recognize that, no matter how hard they try, emotional connection just comes more easily for their partner than it does for them. If they believe in a model of competition, they feel as if they don't measure up. Alternatively, in a spirit of collaboration, they can appreciate their partner's gift for emotions, and they can be open to learning together.

As one person said, "I get it now. It's really so simple: I just listen and respond to what my partner is saying!"

Many have been either numbed out or lost in their elaborate thinking for so long that it takes many repetitions of the Spotlight for them to realize they don't need to avoid or work so hard. They had all the information they needed right in front of them the whole time. They just needed to learn to track their partner emotionally, and their partner needed to learn to stop crossing rivers and jumping off cliffs to throw them off the trail.

This tracking and responding might continue to be easier for one than the other. Partners needn't carry each area of relationship equally. For example, few will be equally adept at the skills and capacities needed to create a meal, prepare the taxes, give a massage, recap the best parts of the movie, navigate the hike without getting lost, and figure out why their toddler is crying. They know they each take the lead in different areas on behalf of the relationship, and they are willing to be influenced as they enjoy a mutual balance of energy.

By experiencing their emotional potency, the formerly withdrawing partner can enter the stream.

One man who had been the more withdrawing partner said he surprised himself by being the one to reach out after years of disconnection:

> With my withdrawal earlier in my life, I didn't even know what I felt. Honestly, I think I would almost go offline, so that I couldn't even respond. Now, I'm just starting to understand what I feel, and I like it a lot. I don't want to go back [to not feeling].

The Challenges of Not Overstepping

For the one who finds it difficult to keep from overstepping, what compels you to that far shore? One woman shares:

> I've tried holding back, but nothing happens. He's plenty happy doing his thing without me. I don't like myself very much when I'm on him all the time, but it's the only way I can get his attention. I'm lonely, and something is better than nothing.

To the one trying to cope with the disconnection by overstepping, I imagine the loneliness and anxiety you feel might be intense at times, and maybe you believe you need to guide your partner to make sure you (and possibly your family) will be okay. But are you really okay if you are slowly losing yourself by settling for less and less?

Many partners try diligently and creatively and just can't get their partner to engage. This leaves them with intense feelings they must learn to self-soothe so they can approach with vulnerable feelings rather than insistent demands.

Vulnerability sounds something like, "When you went out with your friends without asking how that would impact me, I told myself I must not be important to you, and I felt hurt and alone," which is very different from general blaming, such as, "You never think of me. You care more about your friends." Remember, the emotional energy from which you speak matters greatly. Are you speaking from love or fear? And when it's fear (e.g., "I'm afraid I'm not important to you"), naming it and claiming it as your own is a powerful example of holding onto yourself.

When vulnerable revealing happens during the course of therapy, the partner who has stopped overfunctioning can finally stand in confidence for their own relational gifts.

One woman said with an energy of acceptance toward herself and her partner, "I give a lot, and I want a lot."

Hanging onto yourself and expressing your needs vulnerably means you're doing your part in your Revealing role to be the best partner you can be. Some partners will be able to meet you there with generous giving, and some will not.

One man—who tends to pursue—shared that throughout his life, he had a hard time believing he mattered or was worth loving because he was always the more giving partner. After he realized he wanted more and believed he was worth it, he met someone who appreciated his emotional responsiveness and who was able to give the same in return.

Any terms that include the prefixes over- and under- are relative. Where is your functioning as partners relative to each other and the middle stream of your relationship?

Since individuals develop through life at their own pace, what happens when one of you has learned to enter (and not overstep) the stream and the other has not? Can you wake yourselves and each other up? Can you call each other forth? Have you ever considered this learning as being part of the purpose of your relationship?

Undercurrent: How You View the Purpose of Your Relationship

Although you might not have thought of your union in these terms, see if you can relate to the idea of a continuum where, at one end, you hold the view that your relationship as it is now already has the level of intimacy and interaction you want for the long term. You like the status quo and don't desire any additional areas of learning or collaborating together. The other end of the continuum includes a desire for growth and learning within and through the relationship in ways that include more interaction with your partner. Neither end is right or wrong, and any nonabusive agreement is fine as long as you are both consciously agreeing.

Exercise:
If you are interested in learning through the relationship, identify a few specific ways that appeal to you. For example, exploring a new topic, country, culture, or activity, then having meaningful conversations; diving deep into how your past impacts your current life; engaging in personal or spiritual growth; or creating a new vision and tracking your progress together, etc.

When you get specific about growth versus the status quo, are your answers aligned with those of your partner? Perhaps they used to be, but then a negative cycle eroded some of the connection. Or perhaps one of your purposes for being together has ended. Do you need to grieve an old collaboration? Can you cocreate a new purpose?

Undercurrent: Stated Versus Lived Values and Priorities

We want to be attractive to ourselves and others. We develop ideas about who it is good to be or what it is good to be like. For example, *It's good to be married, It's good to take time away from work, It's good to be in a committed relationship,* or *It's good to make my family my priority.*

Stating values, visions, and priorities is important. Equally important is examining how you are living relative to your vision. When you take the time to contemplate these questions, are you living in alignment? Is your partner? Clarity about the differences can help you bridge them.

Undercurrent: The Belief That Men are Less Emotional

I have used the pronouns *they* and *them* throughout the book because I want to expand the conversation about emotions, feelings, connection, and coping styles. I will diverge from that approach briefly to touch on two gender-based beliefs that arise for couples and can cause suffering when hidden as undercurrents. The first is that men have fewer emotions than women. This belief can surface as justification for disconnecting behavior or reduced expectations by either partner. If you adhere to the narrative that men are less emotional, you could deprive yourself and your partner of opportunities for rich connection.

Research supports the finding that, although males are typically socialized from a young age to hide their feelings, males and females do have the same emotions, both in adulthood (Chaplin 2015) and in infancy, where little boys and girls scored the same in their sensitivity and attentiveness to others (Prior et al. 1993).

Given the knowledge of equivalent emotions, how can we bring generous compassion for the ways in which all of us are negatively impacted when men are socialized to suppress their feelings?

Each balanced interaction
brings us closer to the wholeness
of the human experience.

Undercurrent: The Belief That Men Shouldn't Have to Contribute Equally

The second gender-related belief still held by some partners is that men shouldn't have to contribute equally when it comes to the home, family, or emotions. This belief is rarely spoken so clearly, if it is spoken at all. However, when partners begin to consistently engage with their feelings and thoughts regarding these topics, the belief will often surface if present.

In their 2021 book *The 80/80 Marriage*, Nate and Kaley Klemp describe three paradigms of marriage:

1. An 80/80 marriage, in which fights over fairness are left behind by couples who aim higher—much higher—with the radical 80/80 generosity of each partner. This means each partner is striving to give 80 percent.
2. A 50/50 marriage, in which partners attempt to divide responsibilities equally. Although this may sound optimal,

50/50 marriages can lead to a tit-for-tat dynamic and scorekeeping, which wastes energy and creates conflict.

3. An 80/20 marriage, in which the wife is taking care of 80 percent of the household, family, and emotional responsibilities.

Clarity emerges for partners when one reveals that their disinterest in the Moves is caused not by an emotional block but by the belief that men shouldn't have to contribute equally when it comes to the home, family, or emotional life of their relationships. I say this not to discount or minimize the frequency with which a person of any gender feels inequality in their relationship but rather to highlight this particular undercurrent.

Sometimes simply speaking the belief aloud allows one to examine the topic from a new perspective. If after examination one partner wants an 80/20 relationship and the other an 80/80 relationship, then grieving the loss of this difference, as well as related dreams and expectations, creates solid ground for taking the next step, whatever that step may be.

Undercurrent: The Basis of Your Attraction

In his book *Deeper Dating*, Ken Page differentiates between attractions of inspiration and attractions of deprivation. The basis of your attraction to a partner is related to your inner orientation to your core gifts as a person. **Core gifts** are defined as the deepest areas of meaning, tenderness, sensitivity, and creativity within.

If you value your core gifts and seek a partner who does the same, you may be experiencing an attraction of inspiration, where you are encouraged and supported to develop your gifts and share them with the world. If you deny your core gifts and partner with someone who denies them as well, you may be experiencing an attraction of deprivation, which includes the strong pull toward someone because a depriving aspect of the relationship is familiar, even if unhealthy (Page 2014).

Recognizing any familiarity you have with being rejected in your core gift area is important so you can claim or reclaim those gift areas for yourself and begin to kindly and consistently expect the same of your partner.

Sometimes one partner stays with another at least in part because they are trying to work out a core question they have about themself. For example:

- "Am I _____ enough?" If this resonates, you can fill in the blank with the words: kind, worthwhile, lovable, successful, smart, interesting, exciting, fun, attractive, trustworthy, or another word that fits for you.
- "Am I too much?" or "Is my _____ too much?" If this resonates, you can fill in the blank with the words: emotion, intensity, intellect, passion, energy, desire, or another word that fits for you.

In either case, what would it take for you to answer your core question from within and then stand in a new place of self-knowledge as you give and receive? Doing so means hanging onto yourself even as you reach for your partner.

Again, gentleness along the path is essential. Sometimes new awareness is enough, and sometimes it takes many revolutions around the spiral of life to learn the lesson. What if you traveled without shame or blame? What if you sought out others on similar journeys?

Undercurrent: Favoring The Dream Over Reality

Sometimes when one partner is repeatedly frustrated by the other's responses, they come to realize they were in love with the dream of who and how their partner could be rather than the reality of who and how their partner has been and actually is at this time. When your dream of your partner has been chosen in your mind again and again, the longing for that dream with this person can be strong.

 Exercise:
Sit quietly, close your eyes, and see if you are able to contact a deep longing you have about your partner—for example, that they will reach out for affection, stop drinking, start coming home for dinner, seek emotional intimacy, spend less money, be more interested in sex, or ask less of you. By contact, I mean *feel your longing* in the moment rather than just remembering it as something that happened in the past.

Contact your deep longing and then pair that with the current reality, like this:

Yes, I want so much for them to _____, and they don't. This is what's real. They don't.

* * *

We can also validate how difficult it might be for a partner to sense the ways in which their beloved wishes they were different. However, without acknowledging the difference between the longing and what they currently see, they don't have the chance to grieve and live fully into what they do have together.

Any relationship that makes it past the first stages will have disappointments. The key is to grieve these disappointments so they don't become the dynamic tension that holds you together in a negative cycle.

Undercurrent: Secrecy

Along a continuum, "large" secrets (e.g., about your past or about a major relationship dissatisfaction that you're not sharing with your partner) undermine closeness. "Small" secrets (e.g., you really didn't want to have fish for dinner, or you would have turned back there if you were driving) are not problematic and can even be protective of the relationship.

So, when does a secret become an undercurrent? Revealing every thought and feeling that enters our mind is neither healthy nor possible, but when does the harmless omission become an invisible undertow that pulls you away from each other? When does a dissatisfaction need to be spoken in order to preserve the possibility for intimacy? These are big questions. Naturally, partners will have their solitary thoughts, and we all know feelings of closeness in relationships fluctuate.

After attending to the strong emotions that accompany secrets experienced as betrayals—feelings which deserve utmost care and attention—asking, "What function is the secret serving?" can be an illuminating question. If relationship is about growing as a couple *and* as individuals, then what individual need is being addressed by the secret?

In her book *Uncoupling: Turning Points in Intimate Relationships*, Diane Vaughan explores the breakdown of a relationship through the keeping of secrets. In her research, she finds that for couples who ultimately separate, often the impetus is a secret kept by one partner who has little genuine interest in leaving the current relationship but rather is attempting to ease the distress of a personal problem or explore their identity in some important way. Secrets then multiply and become divisive, even though the initial actions were merely intended to ease the distress of a life situation.

As Vaughan writes: "How ironic that our intimate relationships, so often viewed as providing the stable, solid core of our existence [...] are themselves so fragile that they can be undermined by a series of responses to a personal problem— responses intended only to relieve the immediate discomfort of one of the partners."

Well-functioning Spotlight conversations nourish emotional bonds, such that the need for secrets to protect fledgling areas of growth is reduced, and opportunities for positive cycles of responsiveness are enhanced.

> Every undercurrent detected
> strengthens your ability to ride
> the fluctuating waves over time.

Summary

Undercurrents are dangerous. Quickly and quietly, they can pull you away from your desired place. Whether you learn about your relational undercurrents proactively or because you're having trouble connecting with your partner, coming to terms with their existence and impact is crucial to getting where you want to go.

 In Which Direction Lies Your Growth?

- Do you see yourself as overfunctioning or underfunctioning in your relationship? Are you able to stay in the middle stream? What pulls you away?
- How do you view the purpose of your relationship? How has the purpose changed over time?
- In what areas do your stated and lived values align? In what areas is there a gap?
- Do you have undercurrents of gender-related beliefs about responsibilities or the capacity for emotions? Do your beliefs serve you well?
- Do you have an attraction of inspiration or an attraction of deprivation in your relationship?
- Are you keeping secrets? If so, what is the need hidden by the secret? Can that need be brought into the Spotlight?
- Do you recognize any undercurrents not mentioned that are negatively impacting your relationship?

*   *   *

PART IV

GOODNESS OF FIT

———

CHAPTER 12

DATING FIT

How do partners choose each other? What elements are at play?

*   *   *

Your choice of a romantic partner is one of the most import ant decisions you will make in life, as is continuing to choose your partner in a long-term relationship or choosing to end a relationship if you determine you are no longer a good fit.

Throughout the book, you've learned skills of giving, receiving, and revealing that are essential yet rarely taught. You're becoming clearer about cycles, content, undercurrents, and how they interact. Now we will consider all the above and more within the context of the relationship stage.

In this chapter, we explore goodness of fit as it relates to early dating, while the next two chapters focus on the same topic within a primary and long-term relationship. Since these chapters build and reflect upon each other, I recommend reading them in order regardless of your current stage or age. If you and your partner are well past your dating years, you might use the examples as a way to remember and possibly rekindle your early days of loving and learning together.

A Crucible of Development

Dating brings stuff up: insecurities, longings, fears, and judgments, as well as that euphoric feeling you have when all is going well. As if that's not enough, research suggests young adults experience confusion about understanding the type of relationship they are in (e.g., romantic, sexual, both, or not yet either) due to a lack of communication with their partner (Banker et al. 2010).

Despite the challenges, dating provides prime opportunities to learn and practice holding onto yourself and reaching for someone else as you encounter different people and find the one with whom you choose to partner.

Even though you're probably not using the Spotlight Moves with someone you've just met, the energy of that loving beam is available to you wherever you go, and the essence of each Move gives you a way to approach and reflect on your time together.

Dating Fit: Giving

As you think of yourself in the Giving role, what and how are you learning about your date? What would you like to know? Some intention can be helpful. Otherwise, you can get lost in your head about who you think you *should* be or what you think you're *supposed* to say or do.

For instance, sometimes I ask a client, "How did you invite your date to share about themselves?" Then I see the horrified look on their face when they realize they didn't ask at all. They bought into some cultural message that being attractive means impressing someone by squeezing into the conversation every accomplishment and funny story they can recall.

The following conversation highlights the importance of generous giving:

> Two artistic people meet for a third date. One loves poetry, the other, painting.
>
> The poet says to the painter, "I have a Yeats poem I'd like to read to you, if you'd like to hear it."
>
> "Sure, I'd love to," says the painter, while thinking, *Oh no, not another Yeats poem.*
>
> The poet goes on, "I'll tell you my interpretation of it after, and I also looked up some other interpretations."

"Great." *Do they want to know my interpretation?* wonders the painter.

The painter later tells me, "My date reads the poem. My heart sinks as I realize I'm hating it. I don't like the words or the rhythm or anything about it. I remind myself to get curious. Curious about what it means for them and why it touches them. I'm well-behaved and ask something about the poem. They explain, then segue into their relationship with their parents before telling me about their prowess on the basketball court.

"I could have said something about how all this felt but thought, *What's the point?* and decided not to go out with them again."

We can wonder how differently things might have gone if the poet had paused to ask the painter about their interpretation of the poem, or about their art, or about art in general, then taken the time to notice the painter's feelings out loud. We can also wonder what would have happened if the painter had said, "Would you like to hear my interpretation?"

We don't know the poet's story. Maybe they were nervous, and when they're nervous they just talk! Maybe they thought they needed to prove themself in a particular way. Perhaps they weren't genuinely interested in the painter as a person.

Many well-meaning and capable people buy into unfitting versions of who they think they're supposed to be, rather than settling into who they are and trusting that their future partner will be attracted to their authentic self. If you are someone who naturally enjoys a meaningful and mutual exchange, then the Spotlight Moves can help you remember who you are, even when intense emotions and hormones are charging through.

Dating Fit: Revealing

As you imagine being in the Revealing role, what parts of yourself are you making available to your date? Do you trust yourself to share in ways that feel good to you? Are you someone who reveals the tender parts of your heart early? Rarely? Never? Are you comfortable with the pace of your sharing?

Another question to consider is whether or not you are leading with your gifts and the parts of you that most want to be seen, appreciated, and loved. Sometimes a part that's been rejected by important people in the past gets muted for fear of future rejection. Leading with this part can feel risky *and* is an essential dimension for enjoying an attraction of inspiration.

For example, think of an emotionally expressive person being told they were too emotional, so they try to hide that part while still longing to be accepted as their fully feeling self. In a good-fitting relationship, this person will be appreciated for the vibrance and emotional energy they bring.

Another example is someone who is told they are too quiet and not expressive enough. This person might have a rich inner world that longs to be seen and appreciated. If they can learn to regard the many gifts that accompany their personality and being, then they will look for someone who also values these gifts.

Until you lead with the parts of yourself *you* like best, how will your future partner be able to find you?

Dating Fit: Receiving

As you think of yourself in the Receiving role, notice: Is your date offering care and positive attention? If so, are you able to take that in? How easily do you receive? Is there a part of you that wants to have loving light shined on you and a part of you that doesn't? Opening this channel within yourself is an important element of establishing a fluid and flexible relational foundation.

Dating is an ideal time to get a baseline measure of your receiving. Notice what, if anything, shifts as you begin growing closer to someone. As intimacy expands, does it become easier or more difficult to receive?

As partners become the primary person for each other, naturally, expectations build. Keeping an eye on your expectations and noticing which ones might echo back to other primary people in your life helps you recognize which are appropriate to carry forward to your partner, given your values and intentions. This is where your Adult and non-Adult parts might have some conflicting views. The key is learning when and how to draw upon the different parts of yourself.

"I delight in being a child when it's appropriate to be a child. I delight in being a wise old man when it's appropriate to be a wise old man. Think of all I can be! I am every age, up to my own."

—MORRIE SCHWARTZ, *TUESDAYS WITH MORRIE*

Whether you are reading this in your twenties, your sixties, or beyond, you have the opportunity to delight in and learn from all your ages and stages.

How Do I Feel with This Person?

An integral question to be asking yourself while dating is: How do *I* feel with this person? You can easily get sidetracked and overlook yourself with questions such as: What did *they* think of me? Am I the kind of person *they're* looking for? How can I be more attractive to *them*?

It makes sense you would have all these wonderings, *and* remembering to ask yourself how *you* feel can reorient you to your inner wisdom.

Notice your nervous system before you create any meaning about what it's telling you. Notice your heart rate, your breathing, your chest, your stomach, and any other parts that call for attention. In general, ask yourself: Is my nervous system calm, soothed, and relaxed? Is it anxious and agitated in some way? Keep noticing moment to moment.

Notice your thoughts in general. Are there many, or just a few? Is there an ease to being together? Are you trying hard to make something happen? Do you ever shut down due to overwhelm?

Exercise:
- What do I notice inside of me while my date is _____?
  Does my nervous system react with calm or anxious signals?
- What do I notice inside of me while I am _____ with my date? Does my nervous system react with calm or anxious signals?

Knowing how you feel can be harder than it sounds, especially if you've spent many years or a lifetime being strongly influenced by what others want you to be, feel, or do.

Noticing your emotions is the first step. Listening for your own wisdom about them is another. In this area, you may benefit from working with a therapist and with practices that enhance your mindful awareness.

What's My Vision?

This early stage of relationship can help you hone in on your values, priorities, and the characteristics of a person you think you would enjoy being with. As one woman shared:

> I never knew what real love or healthy relationships should look like. I didn't have a good example. So, when I was young, I thought, *Okay, this person has a good job. They'll come home every night.* I was checking these boxes... but I never considered what I needed from someone as a partner and a friend. I hadn't thought about mutual support.

A clear vision that reflects your values gives you some grounding to return to when emotions run high. Emotions are important as information. However, as Robert Fritz highlights in *Creating: A Practical Guide to the Creative Process and How to Use It to Create Anything—A Work of Art, a Relationship, a Career or a Better Life,* visions are realized when basing your life on your choices and being clear about the difference between your vision and your current reality. Carefully considering your vision of a good-fitting mate can help you recognize the person when you meet them.

This conscious process can also ward off the impulse to end a relationship prematurely. Did your younger self decide there is a particular feature or characteristic that your person must or must not have? Are you expecting to experience a particular feeling?

For example, do you find yourself thinking any of these thoughts?

- They are too heavy/thin, short/tall, brown-eyed/blue-eyed, etc.
- They are just too nice. I want someone who is edgy.
- I thought I would feel _____ (e.g., intense butterflies like with a high school crush).

Exploring where your younger images and expectations have come from helps you decide which ones to keep. I'm guessing you wouldn't want to let go of someone who could be a good fit for you as a true partner simply because they don't match an image you adopted in childhood or adolescence.

Possible Selves

Possible selves are visions, fears, and hopes of who you might become. One of the benefits of dating is learning how various parts of you can be called forth by different relationships and experiences. While it simply isn't possible to know how you will grow and develop, spending some time bringing your possible selves into view can be beneficial. As psychologist Hazel Markus and scholar Paula Nurius write:

"Positive possible selves can be exceedingly liberating because they foster hope that the present self is not immutable."

"At the same time, negative possible selves can be powerfully imprisoning because their associated affect and expectations may stifle attempts to change or develop."

What do you notice about your positive and negative possible selves while dating? How do you envision yourself and your life with one person, and then how do you envision differently with another?

A parent notes how the friendships and dating relationships of her adult children bring out different parts of them, and how they bring out different aspects in their friends and romantic partners. One father told her he loved who his daughter was ("self-confident and happy") with her adult child.

This parent also reflected on her own relationships, noting people who weren't a good fit for her. She shared examples of "[people] who made me self-conscious about my weight, which resulted in my having unhealthy behaviors, or people who brought out my Type A personality and made me anxious. With some, I ended up caring too much [about] what they thought. Not because they were bad or did anything wrong, but because of what they brought out *in me*."

She speaks beautifully to the ideas of goodness of fit and possible selves. We all have different parts of ourselves, aspects to our personalities, and varying capacities. By checking in with yourself and your own experience, you can notice what parts of you are being called forth by your dating partner.

Intrapsychic Fit

Another awareness-building idea to consider is that of *intrapsychic fit*, which describes how we're drawn to people with personality characteristics that are a complement to our own. We are attracted to the ability of the other person to express themself or handle their life in ways that tend to be more challenging for us. This dynamic is considered to be a powerful and unconscious element in choosing a mate and one that remains intact in the relationship until a big event (e.g., having children, changing careers, losing a parent, etc.) challenges the ability of each individual and the partnership to adapt (Zentman 2013).

This dynamic often becomes noticeable for couples when one partner now despises some aspect of the other that they once cherished. Consider these examples: "I loved that you were confident in the world. Now, all you want is to be out all the time," or "I loved your emotion. Now, can you tone it down a little?" or "I was drawn to your steadiness. Now, I wonder if you have feelings at all." In each of these expressions, the once adored characteristic likely was (or is) less developed or less accessible in the once adoring partner.

While you can't possibly know how you will grow, change, or influence each other if you were to become partners, the enhancing question while dating at this stage is:

Does my dating partner have a gift or capability I admire and also struggle with?

Once you have the awareness, you can then consciously choose whether or not to develop that aspect within yourself and appreciate the complementary balance from your partner.

Do I Want to Go Out with This Person Again?

Sometimes there can be pressure from within or without to know more than whether you want to go out just one more time, as if saying yes to another date somehow commits you to a lifetime together. You may also feel this pressure due to the all-too-common, flawed logic of the cultural message that you'll be leading that person on if you say yes to another date and then say no down the road.

An internalized message that you're not to disappoint might keep you from speaking freely. In situations involving abuse or coercion, I recommend you seek trusted others, including professionals who can help. For our purposes, the potentially illuminating idea is: If you don't trust that you can say no whenever you need to, then your yes doesn't have your full support either.

A yes is meaningful only when you are fully free to say no.

If you are not interested in another date, then I encourage you to be direct and clear, even if your date begins to signal an emotionally reactive reply, as was the case in the following story:

One person shared, following the end of a first date in which they decided to decline the offer of another, that their date then yelled, "Why were you so nice to me? You smiled, and asked about me, and laughed at what I said."

Afterward the person who declined wondered, "Should I have not been nice?"

Not being yourself for fear of hurting someone's feelings down the road can't possibly work for you because then you're not leading with your gifts, and the person with whom you do have goodness of fit might not recognize you. The invitation in this example is to willingly bear the accusation of betrayal while staying in the Adult part of yourself. Remember, the Adult speaks the facts, even if the facts are about feelings.

For anyone who has ever reactively said something similar to, "Why were you so nice to me?" it makes sense that being interested in someone who isn't interested in you can be frustrating, sad, and maybe lead to an empty feeling. All kinds of unhelpful thoughts could get mixed in with your experience. If you are having trouble connecting with people you are interested in, I encourage you to find someone to help you explore the questions above about how you give, receive, and reveal on your dates. Perhaps you need to work through a block or learn a skill that would help your best qualities become more visible for a fitting partner.

If you date for any amount of time in your life, you will likely be the one to decline another date and, at some point, be the one who is declined. Being on both sides of these decisions has all the makings of compassion for our human experience. For the most part, we've all said *yes* and we've all said *no*. We're all seeking goodness of fit.

The Expectations of Others

While I have talked throughout this book about the *inner* of you as an individual and the *in-between* of your relationship as a way to focus on these particular dynamics, the layers of environment and culture need attention too.

As you bring curiosity to the cultural expectations and norms of your friends, family, institutions, the media, and society in general, which do you want to adopt and which would you like to try leaving behind? I say *try* because we as people are wired for belonging. We need each other, and the fear of disconnection that can come with making a different choice can be immense.

Oftentimes a cultural lens you've adopted thus far will be a match for your values and visions, and oftentimes it won't. Even if you choose expectations, beliefs, or behaviors that you recognize are *not* a good fit for all or some part of you, I invite you to bring compassion to this choice. Great value exists in being clear with yourself and a few trusted others. For example: "I want to make a different choice, *and* I'm afraid to make a different choice." Holding both aspects side by side is expansive.

One person shared that they didn't want to kiss their date at the end of the night, and they also didn't say no because they didn't want to be a problem. Rather than reject their date, they rejected themselves. Many have been conditioned to be polite and take responsibility for the other person's feelings.

Speaking their thoughts to me later, they shared, "I wanted to say no, but I was afraid to say no." Then we changed the *but* to an *and*, and they slowly spoke the new sentence, "I wanted to say no, *and* I was afraid to say no." By feeling their feelings and holding both truths together, they found the entryway to self-compassion and the courage to square their shoulders toward the direction of their growth.

Summary

"The possession of knowledge does not kill the sense of wonder and mystery. There is always more mystery."

—ANAÏS NIN

The knowledge you gain by paying attention to your vision, possible selves, intrapsychic fit, the flow of giving and receiving, how you feel with someone in the moment, and the expectations of others prepares you for the mystery that awaits.

 In Which Direction Lies Your Growth?

- How did you invite your date to share about themselves?
- Are you revealing the parts of yourself you like best?
- Do you know what qualities and characteristics fit your vision of a partner?
- Have you taken on any expectations of your family or friends that you'd rather leave behind?
- As you reflect on this chapter, what intentions are you drawn toward?

CHAPTER 13

PRIMARY FIT

——

Do I fit you?
Do you fit me?
Do we fit *we*?

*   *   *

Settling into a primary relationship is where the rubber meets the road, so to speak. This is where an intentional way to talk about your thoughts and feelings can help you find balance and build a strong foundation.

One challenge for this stage is that as you become emotionally connected as primary partners, the freedom you felt with each other early on might be dissipating. You might start to share less of yourself from fear of losing the connection you have. In a way, revealing before you're attached and primary with each other is easier. You're both on your best behavior, and neurotransmitters are impacting you with an intensity that rivals being on a stimulant such as cocaine (Wu 2017).

During this phase of relationship, obsessiveness and idealization gradually decrease as dopamine and serotonin levels return to normal. Simultaneously, increasing levels of oxytocin enhance bonding, calmness, immune function, physical and mental health, and more mature forms of love (Powell 2018). Fears will inevitably keep popping up, and with them opportunities for you and your partner to become secure sources of comfort for one another.

Building upon the suggestions of the previous chapter, we're going to explore additional topics that are especially relevant for this stage of relationship, as well as ways Spotlight Moves can help you zoom in for clarity about your goodness of fit.

Values and Assumptions

By intentionally focusing on your partner, you'll be discovering what matters to them and what they value—as well as how your values align in the following ways: intellectually, physically, sexually, emotionally, spiritually, financially, socially, and with regard to family, lifestyle, travel for work and play, and the way they view the purpose of their relationship.

For a standardized approach, the Prepare/Enrich tool for premarital and married couples (Olson-Sigg et al. 2008) includes research-based feedback and coaching, and it identifies ten categories to explore:

- Communication
- Conflict resolution
- Partner style and habits
- Financial management
- Leisure activities
- Affection and sexuality
- Family and friends
- Children and parenting
- Relationship roles
- Spiritual beliefs

Partners considering having children may want to read *The Defining Decade*, in which Dr. Meg Jay, a clinical psychologist, identifies parenthood as the most significant before and after event of a couple's life and offers a relevant and helpful set of questions for readers to consider.

After taking some time to explore your own values and curiously listening for those of your partner, I invite you to ask yourself: How much am I longing for our values to match? And how much do they match right now? By whatever lens you choose to consider values, be as sincere with yourself as you can be.

> Love consists of seeing someone clearly—seeing them as they are, rather than as we want them to be.

In the promise of a growing relationship, we make assumptions about what the other person thinks, feels, and desires, while looking past or forgetting to ask what they actually express as their thoughts, feelings, and desires. We think we know *and*, naturally, we all have blind spots.

> One person shared a story in which she thought moving in with her partner would mean they would have more sex. Turns out, *he* thought moving in together would mean they would settle down and have less sex. They were each making assumptions about what moving in together would mean.

We can often detect clues as to which direction partners are leaning on particular topics. We don't investigate these clues because we're sure what we think is accurate. Many times, we don't even know we have assumptions until we're forced by a life event or asked by an important person to examine them.

Examples of assumptions include:

- When we have a family, we'll spend more time together.
- When we're married, life will be easier.
- When we blend our families, we will parent each other's children.
- I will work while you stay home with the kids, then you will work while I stay home with the kids.
- You will embrace my religious faith and practices.
- Life is short! We will work just enough to pay the monthly bills.
- Life is short! We will work long hours now so we can retire early.
- We will always drink and party the way we do now.
- One day, our parents will move in with us.

You might especially want to consider values and assumptions related to your priorities. For example, your possible selves might be very ambitious, valuing a vibrant partnership, soaking up time with your kids, excelling at a high-pressure job, volunteering for several organizations, enjoying ample downtime, and hiking with your friends every weekend. These could all be entirely possible. And just in case they're not, which ones do you value most?

Every choice means other choices can't be made. Which ones are core for you?

The Spotlight Moves can help you explore your own assumptions and have a conversation with your partner about theirs.

Revealing at This Stage

There's a common belief that the couples who overlook their frustrations and disconnections with each other are happier and stay together longer. Yet research of married partners suggests the opposite correlation. The couples who have a lower tolerance for disconnection and therefore talk through even minor dissatisfactions until both are satisfied are happier and less likely to divorce (Fry 2015).

This stage of becoming primary with each other is a key time for establishing relational templates, including one for talking through dissatisfactions and disconnections. We have a tendency to repeat what we know or swing to the opposite extremes unless we consciously choose our preferred path.

In the examples below, see if you can identify your typical style of communicating and where you learned it, as well as the way you would prefer to communicate when you feel anger or frustration, sadness, or anxiety. Gentleness with yourself is an important posture as you identify your style. Being able to say, "Yes, I do behave like this, and I'd like to do it differently," is a courageous act.

Anger/Frustration:

- **Acted out and placed upon your partner:** You are the lowest of the low, and it's your job to make me feel better!
- **Directed inward and not expressed:** I'm angry, but I dare not say it. This will blow over.
- **Disowned and projected:** I'm not angry. You're the one who is angry.
- **Direct and vulnerable:** I'm so angry with you right now. What just happened brought up a lot of frustration and hurt for me.

Sadness:

- **Acted out and placed upon your partner:** You don't care about me. If you cared about me, I wouldn't be sad. Please, make things better for me.
- **Directed inward and not expressed:** I'm sad, but I'm afraid to tell you because then I'll have to _____.
- **Disowned and projected:** I'm not sad. You're the sad one.
- **Direct and vulnerable:** I'm sad. What's between us is bringing up sadness. I feel it inside like a weight on my heart.

Anxiety:

- **Acted out and placed upon your partner:** You make me so anxious. I'm counting on you to fix everything so I never have this feeling.
- **Directed inward and not expressed:** I'm anxious. What's wrong with me? I shouldn't feel this way.
- **Disowned and projected:** I'm not anxious, but look at you. You're a mess!
- **Direct and vulnerable:** I am anxious about this, and this is what that feels like...

What makes navigating these and other feelings so difficult at times? Parker Palmer, author, educator, and activist, teaches that "there is no way to be human without having one's heart broken."

The term *heartbreak* may sound intense, yet how else can we explain the intensely negative reactions partners can experience with one another? Dr. Palmer describes the epicenter of the pain:

> There is no way to be human without having one's heart broken, but there are at least two ways for the heart to break [...]. The heart can be broken into a thousand shards, sharp-edged fragments that sometimes become shrapnel aimed at the source of our pain [...] or *broken open* into largeness of life, into greater capacity to hold one's own and the world's pain and joy.

As long as we're breaking, how might we break open into this greater capacity? Would we have more compassion for ourselves and each other if we could feel for our own heartbreak rather than acting blindly from it?

In your relationship, the closer you get to revealing thoughts and feelings directly and vulnerably, the more you'll expand into this greater capacity where your Giving partner has a better chance of finding you.

How Much to Share?

In which direction lies the growth? If speaking up has been difficult, what would it be like to speak more? If holding your own counsel has been challenging, could you practice this? How do you cultivate your gifts while gently leaning into your areas of growth?

The terms we use, such as willing, vulnerable, and direct, are subjective and relative. As you think of yourself in these ways, what is the range of your sweet spot as a person and as a couple? What is your range, and how can you move together within that range? What is the concert of your partnership?

Some partners want to reveal nearly everything that bothers them. Some don't want to reveal much of anything due to fear of intimacy or fear of making waves, or perhaps because their areas of giftedness are solitary and they leave little time for interaction relative to someone who thrives on numerous intimate exchanges. The exercise below can help one get closer to understanding the motivation beneath their impulses, tendencies, and choices.

<u>Exercise:</u>

Examine your thoughts as they come into your mind and ask yourself which ones are based on love and which are based on fear. Try not to parse them. If there is any fear present, then this is a fear thought. Identifying the nature of your thoughts can help you act with compassion toward the fearful parts of yourself as you decide what to vulnerably share with your partner.

What Not to Say—Unless You're Certain

Deep hurts stem from statements such as, "I'm done," or, "I can't do this anymore," because the one hearing the statement might understandably interpret this as their partner saying the relationship is over, although the one speaking the statement might more specifically mean, "I hate this feeling. I know we're going to end up in this exact same place again, and I feel helpless to stop it." If partners don't know about cycles, strategies for addressing them, and ways to identify and share their more tender thoughts and emotions, then the feeling of helplessness can ramp up the intensity.

Threats to the relationship often become attachment wounds that stay with partners and are difficult to heal without a lot of care and attention. If these kinds of wounds have occurred between you, and you are having a difficult time reconnecting, I recommend working with a therapist to heal the moments when your sense of security together was lost or broken.

Time-out!

Calling a partner time-out is imperative when you notice that either of you are becoming over- or under-activated and losing your sense of *we* in an interaction. Agreeing upon your time-out terms in a calm moment, rather than in the middle of an argument, greatly increases your chances of success. Terms often include:

- A standard amount of time (e.g., twenty minutes, or an hour, or whatever length of time you find optimal). Any amendment to the length of the time-out requires full agreement from both partners.
- Agreement that either of you can call the time-out when you believe the break would be beneficial. Perhaps you could think of yourselves as co-coaches for the same team in a championship game. When there is an important play coming up, you call the time-out so the players can stretch, get a drink of water, and remember their game plan.
- Agreement to immediately honor the time-out when it's called.
- Agreement to take responsibility for returning yourself to a calm emotional state during your time-out. How? Relive a positive memory. Review your Moves and think about who will be in which role following your time-out. Or— prepare to have some favorite reading material nearby. Researchers have found that the exercise of reading a magazine can reduce the emotional and physiological flooding of partners who are in conflict (Gottman and Gottman, 2018).

- Optional: a playful time-out ritual such as a fun code word to replace "time-out" or an agreement to wear the funny hats you made for your post-time-out returns to each other.

How is Your Partner Doing in Their Giving Role?

As you reveal your inner world, you also notice how well your partner shines the Spotlight on you. Skills such as inviting and validating can be learned. If you would like to be on the receiving side of these skills one day, then this stage of relationship is a key time to notice:

- Do we learn well together?
- Does my partner have the energy and willingness to engage?
- Do we influence each other?
- Can my partner admit, "I want to learn, *and* I don't know how yet"? Or are they promising this to me in the future, or criticizing me for my feelings and desires?
- How does their response feel to me?

Anxious Attachment Voices

Do you ever experience the inner voice of an anxious attachment by thinking, *I want too much, or I'll never do better [than the person I'm with now], or I'll bet if I broke up with my partner, then they'd become who I want but with someone else?*

Some people who have these thoughts secretly fear that if their partner found more happiness with someone else, then they would lose. That would prove there's something unlovable about them. If you have these secret fears, would you like to address them with a trusted person? Once you know deep down you are lovable, you'll more easily find a partner who positively mirrors these qualities back to you.

The Negativity Bias

Just as positive dreams can overlay reality, negative dreams can too. These dreams are the fears you have about your partner or your relationship that don't match reality at this time. These fears ensnare some part of you, speaking words such as:

- I know they'll leave;
- I know they won't be supportive of me; or
- Here we go again. I'll never be enough.

 Exercise:
Sit quietly, close your eyes, and see if you are able to contact the fear you have about your partner. By contact, I mean *feel your fear* in the moment rather than just remembering it as something that happened in the past. Contact your fear and then pair that with the current reality, like this:

I am so scared they will (or won't) _____ , *and* as I look at them right now, _____ feels true.

*   *   *

If you become aware you are overlaying fear where it doesn't belong, the combination of inner work and couples work can be transformational. Remember, you don't need to go it alone when you have a partner who is willing to let your relationship be a healing force for you both.

Negotiating

When partners have differing ideas about how to solve a problem or make a decision, I suggest negotiating collaboratively until both partners are satisfied with the outcome. This stance places you on the same team with the same goal, rather than facing off in competition or settling for a compromise neither of you is happy with. One person shared the following about negotiating in her marriage:

> I believe if you want to get your needs met, you have to be willing to ask. You have to be able and willing to confront. My partner is very good at negotiating for certain things that are really important to him, like saving money. But I'm very comfortable with confronting things in general. So, he will lob something out, and then I will come back with a counteroffer. There is a give and take that has to happen in order for both of us to feel like we're getting our needs met.
>
> We keep going back and forth and adding on or subtracting until we find something that fits for both of us. Or one person decides, "Right now this isn't as important for me." Then maybe the next time an issue arises, we refer back and might say, "Okay, so

you kind of got your way there, and this is now really important to me." There's a lot of that.

When I asked how they keep resentment from building, she replied:

I think the conversation is always going. We're just making sure that each other's happiness is as important as our own. We make sure we're both getting something out of it. Otherwise, we could easily be resentful.

We also try to bring humor, and we've learned when to stop talking about something. When a negotiation gets too heated, or too emotional, then we agree to revisit another time when we're both feeling more grounded or even just more rested. Which isn't always easy, because when we're *in it*, we each want to get our point across!

They operate with the collaborative principle:

If something matters to you, it matters to me.

Sometimes couples cognitively agree with this principle, yet they haven't developed the awareness and skills needed to negotiate collaboratively. In her article titled, "The Right Way to Negotiate with Your Partner," Catherine Aponte notes that win-win collaborations include, but aren't limited to, the following characteristics:

- Each partner is able to identify wants and desires;
- Each partner is willing to negotiate their wants and desires; and

- Each partner can explain what is important about the stated wants and desires.

With your trusted partner holding the beam steady, the repetition of the Moves provides opportunities to keep practicing for win-win outcomes.

Summary

During this unique stage of your relationship, strategies such as examining assumptions, exploring values, communicating vulnerably and directly, and negotiating collaboratively help partners become clearer about their own and their partner's interest, capacity, skill, and energy for giving and receiving/revealing.

 In Which Direction Lies Your Growth?

- What do you value, and what do you value most? What would an observer identify as your values if they saw your actions but couldn't hear your words?
- How do your values match up with those of your partner?
- How many assumptions can you uncover? Do you want to check them out with your partner?
- In what ways do you communicate your anger, sadness, and anxiety? Do you connect with the experience or idea of heartbreak?
- Do you ever experience an anxious attachment voice?
- Do you sometimes have a negative vision of your partner that doesn't line up with what you see in your present

moments? How can you get help sorting out this important information?

- Think back on a time (one memory) when you negotiated. How did it go? Did you go back and forth with offers and counteroffers until you were both satisfied? Or do you have another way to negotiate for win-win results?

CHAPTER 14

DEEPENING FIT

"If you want to go fast, go alone; if you want to go far, go together."
—Author Unknown

✳   ✳   ✳

The time and experience of a long-term relationship provide you and your partner with ongoing opportunities to make the modifications and repairs needed for the functionality, fun, and safety of your relationship. As with retrofitting a house, some structural work to the foundation might also be needed to replace or repurpose the crumbled, splintering, and broken elements with new updated materials.

Think of all the character and memories in an old house. If enough are good, then the retrofit is well worth the cost, and you'll have a beautiful new home together.

Even if your future as a couple has never been in question, your new insights and experiences can enhance the ways you think, feel, and talk about your relationship. Creating more positive memories adds to the loving loop of associations

between you and helps crystallize the wisdom you want to pass on to the next generation.

The Fabric of Us

When you become a couple, you begin to weave your two individual strands into a fabric that includes your people (family, friends, neighbors, and coworkers), your places (where you've traveled and lived together), your practical lives (home, pets, jobs, finances, hobbies, and care of others), your practices (physical, emotional, sexual, and spiritual), your memories, and more. Often people don't realize all the ways they've become *home* for each other until a death or divorce alters their world.

All these connections, memories, loves, and comforts make the vulnerability of this chapter unique. If you or your partner determine you're not a good enough fit and you do not wish to rebuild, there can be much to lose. Given this, the clarity that can be found via the Spotlight becomes even more important because decisions made in an emotional fog of confusion, guilt, shame, or low self-worth might later be regretted.

If you have been unsure of your goodness of fit, the experience of reaching the same stuck point again and again, while potentially frustrating, can also be liberating when you begin to see and understand the dynamics at play. In the struggle, you have the opportunity to work through any illusions you hold that things are different than what you see.

(What was longed for) – (Reality) = (What you have to grieve)

Seeing where and how you are each giving and receiving allows you to lean more fully into gratitude for all the ways in which you are a good fit and, likewise, lean fully into your grief for the ways in which you are not. While the word *grief* may sound daunting, this grief process often helps partners strengthen their bonds and deepen their recommitments.

Willingness

Is there currently a goodness of fit for your relationship? The first step toward knowing is a willingness to look and see.

One man I interviewed spoke about willingness as related to the fit in his relationship. He posed the following questions:

Do we have willingness to even look at where there is and where there isn't a good fit? And when there isn't, is there a willingness for us to look for a change opportunity? Or create the fit? Do we want that? And are we willing to do the work to get there?

When I asked further for his definition of *willing*, he responded that for him willingness includes an acceptance that there is an ill-fitting situation as well as an action to acknowledge his part and to say:

> I'm aware of it. I accept that that's what I do. That it's not outside of me. And that I want something. There's a desire to be closer... It's exploration. It's curiosity. It's open and honest. It requires a lot of humility. It means knowing you're going to get it wrong. It requires a lot of trust.

Within the context of couples therapy, research supports that "a willingness to engage" and make use of therapeutic services is linked with positive outcomes (Kysely et al. 2020). Whether or not a couple is engaged in therapy, the willingness of a partner can be difficult to discern. What do you see in yourself and in your partner when you look via your AWE?

What If Only One Is Reaching for More Connection?

Many wonder if change is possible when only one partner is actively working on the relationship or when one partner is giving more energy than the other. Yes, change is still possible. If one part of the system changes, then by definition the system overall will change in some way.

Partners who decide to work on the relationship solo embrace opportunities to:

- Listen for how they are impacting their partner;
- Learn more deeply how their partner is impacting them;
- Find ways to regulate their own emotions; and
- Clean up their side of the street behaviorally.

After taking on these challenges themselves, they are often able to reengage with their partner, this time while holding onto their own wants, needs, and worth in ways they might not have been able to before. Sometimes the efforts of one create enough of a shift for both to reconnect.

And when partners are not able to reconnect, I like to remind the one who made the solo effort: Just because your partner couldn't or didn't receive you doesn't mean you didn't live your side of the relationship well enough. Relationships are cocreations, which is easy to forget if you learned to take on extra relational responsibilities early in life.

A Willingness to Grieve

According to grief expert Laurie Roberts, PhD, "One of the primary reactions to a significant loss is the feeling of losing control—and we people like to have control."

In an attempt to gain control, it's not uncommon to become smaller under the weight of grief, to stop dreaming, or to limit your life. When we are willing, our grief points the way to the hurt places that need attention. Where we have strong and difficult emotions we often experience pain, and under that pain, deep care about something that has been lost—a trust, a dream, or a closeness. Reconnecting with deep caring reawakens the heart toward compassion for oneself and others and compels the imagination toward updated visions.

> Where pain pushes us toward change, vision pulls. Yet even the most longed-for changes and visions can fail due to an inability to grieve.

When you become clear about your hurts and losses, what aspects need your gentle attention? Are you able to feel your grief? Since the accompanying sadness and helplessness can be difficult to allow, partners often more readily identify *resentment*. Resentment, while understandable, is a thought or series of thoughts about rightness and wrongness that often results in being stuck and enduring additional pain, whereas grief is an organic process that tills the ground for something new to grow.

Susan Cain, author of *Bittersweet: How Sorrow and Longing Make Us Whole*, speaks to the relational aspect of grief as she writes: "Sorrow and tears are one of the strongest bonding mechanisms we have."

Grieving losses throughout life—whether of loved ones, relationships, jobs, or dreams—is an important way to keep your heart open to yourself and your partner.

While paths of healing and restoration abound, the questions of how, how much, and the timing, we must admit, are unknown. Similarly, with an abundance of love in the world, perhaps part of the mystery is the way in which love falls short where we've expected it and appears where we might not have thought to look.

Once you've found a spacious, loving container to hold your grief while it's cooking, you can begin to acknowledge the ingredients with your willing partner. For example:

"I care about you and us,
and
I'm also angry and sad,
and
I want to be able to receive all the ways you're trying now.
And
I can't yet…
and
I hope you don't stop trying."

Rarely is there one definitive statement. Using the word *and* can help your voice find its way.

<u>Exercise:</u>
Imagine the strength of your feelings on a scale of zero to ten. Now allow your mind to go to a memory of a difficult moment with your partner—one where the feeling you have doesn't get higher than a five or a six. How do you feel now as you reexperience that one memory?

If the moment has been fully resolved, you will feel clear and calm even though you experienced distress back at the time of the event. If your nervous system often feels activated or jumbled and you can't get what feels like a clear read, then notice this with your own caring presence. This alone can be transformative.

If you're having a hard time knowing how you feel or your feelings shift frequently, you might be tempted to rush past the discomfort. Being able to identify, understand, and trust your inner signals is important. If you're having difficulty with any of these or if your negative feelings are stronger than a six, I encourage you to find a professional to help—someone with whom you feel safe, so you can become acquainted with your inner guidance and wisdom. While you can take many paths to learning in these ways, when the past pain or trauma has occurred in the relationship, often the most robust healing happens in the relationship as well.

A Willingness for Gratitude

Often the good memories are harder to access while the hurt is intense, *and* we need our gratitude. Alternating between the heights of your grief and your gratitude expands your inner windows of tolerance and compassion for all life's experiences.

Alongside the grief, what do you appreciate about your partner or your relationship?

Exercise:
Allow your mind to go to a memory of one of the best moments with your partner. How does your body feel? Keep zooming in on the best moment of this one memory and let any good feelings spread all through you. What's a positive belief about yourself as a person as you are reliving this memory? (Examples of positive beliefs: I belong. I'm okay. I'm worth loving. I'm safe. I can make choices.) Hold the positive belief in your mind as you focus on the details of the memory. Continue as long as the exercise is enhancing the positive for you.

Building your inner library of positive moments and reliving them fully creates emotions that act like medicine to heal pain and doubt.

* * *

As you continue to explore your goodness of fit, hold the expressions of both your grief and gratitude together. Both are powerful healing agents that can return you to the heart of your connection.

Similar to the process mentioned above, Laurie Roberts shared an exercise she facilitates with clients who are struggling with any stressful, traumatic, or unwanted images. While she specifically focuses on images related to the death of a loved one, the process is the same for any distressing memory. In the exercise, she has the client see the unwanted image in their mind, relive their senses from that moment—everything they can see, smell, hear, and taste—and then notice their related feelings and sensations in the present moment.

She then directs them to change their focus to a positive image of their loved one, and then to relive that moment fully with their senses and related feelings.

By directing clients back and forth between the negative image and the positive, by adding bilateral tapping as is used with EMDR, and by reassuring them they don't need to let go of the negative image until they are ready, most people successfully release the negative image such that it no longer appears as an intruder in their minds.

If you are stuck with unwanted images related to stressful or traumatic moments with your partner, I recommend finding a professional to help you through this process. Creating and enjoying new positive moments together will be much more possible once the traumatic aspects of the old memories have resolved and healed.

A Willingness to Step Forward with What You Know

One woman shares her story:

> Early in my marriage, I was complaining about all the ways I didn't feel partnered, and then I remember thinking, *Wait a minute. I'm not partnering well for him either.* At that point, I made a real commitment to show up as the best possible partner I could be. I did that for many years, and then when we had another round of him telling me what was wrong with me, I got really clear with myself and what I wanted.

I decided I'm not going to beg. I'm not going to plead. I'm not going to bargain. I'm just going to say, "This is what I want. If you'd like to give it to me, great. If you don't want to give it to me, then let's not do this anymore." His answer was, "Let's not do this anymore."

Now I find myself in a new relationship with someone where there's so much flow... of partnership, of playfulness, of actually being loved and adored for who I am. I mean, we fight, and we upset each other, and we struggle. But the contrast is so striking that I do want to let people know goodness of fit matters. There are people who want to play the way you want to play, and if you can find one of them, it's a lot better than working so hard—working so hard for so little.

A Willingness for Forgiveness

Like so many aspects of a relationship, forgiveness can be intended but not forced. For those of us who have ever done something we wish we hadn't (or *not* done something we wish we had) or been on the receiving side of either of these—forgiveness, when and if that can be cultivated, often brings peace and compassion.

When there has been an injury in a relationship, often, partners make promises that the same type of injury won't be repeated. Promises become reliable when they are based on some reality in the past. Until that point, especially if secrecy was involved, healing happens more often when the one who broke the trust is willing to be open to their partner's feelings and questions.

As one person shared:

> I can't believe I did what I did. I was so fixated on this
> other person that I blew up my marriage and hurt the
> person I love most. I also hurt myself because that's
> not who I am. Now I worry I can't get the trust back.
> I've said it's okay to talk about what happened as many
> times as needed, even though it kills me every time.

When the right combination of elements is present, and both
partners are able to reveal their pain and shine loving care
and attention on each other as often as needed, the feeling
in the room is one that is unique. In some detectable way,
the pain that was once somewhat distinct for each person
becomes fully shared, and held, and healed.

*   *   *

In long-term relationships, you may judge your younger self
or your partner's younger self harshly for not having the
wisdom you have now. Often, you may feel pressure to have
known something before you knew it. To expect yourselves
to be able to see around every turn adds undue strain and
can create a fair amount of misery. Committing and recom-
mitting to someone means you take their hand and take a
leap. It's a leap because, although you can set your intentions,
you can't possibly know how you'll feel, change, or choose in
the future, let alone how your partner will.

What you can get closer to is the truth of your experience right now.

This becomes more possible for all of us when we can show up in critical moments as our Adult selves to drive the cars of our lives—with our inner children strapped safely in the back!

When partners are able to forgive their younger selves, not only as individuals (i.e., "I forgive you, and I forgive me") but also as a couple (i.e., "I forgive us"), they learn and accept that they were a good-enough fit at one point in time, and they couldn't have known then how they would change and grow. With this new compassion for themselves, they can more freely make their next move.

New Foundation(s)

"Each of you is perfect the way you are… and you can use a little improvement."

—SHUNRYU SUZUKI

We're Doing This!

One couple shared:

> We struggled with big fights and long silences. At times it felt impossible, but we've realized we need to work on our love every day because we see the world differently.
>
> Could this have happened years ago? We will never know. I'm grateful I couldn't settle for the status quo. I insisted we find a new way—or divorce. I became more assertive, which was good growth for me. My spouse wanted to stay together and made some changes. Now we are in a new phase. We were able to resurrect a loving relationship.

They weathered storms and repaired their foundation, *and* they know the upkeep continues. They don't fear future renovations. They have positive memories of the loving that can happen when they hold and reach.

> Even when your foundation has been repaired, your intention, attention and ongoing maintenance are still needed!

One form of as-needed maintenance is the vulnerable reveal-ing of uncertainties that can arise when one feels threatened in some way due to their partner's growth or change. Consider these examples of vulnerable revealing and correspond-ing requests: "Since you're confident in the world now, I'm worried you won't need me anymore. I know this is about me, and I'd like to check it out with you too," or "Since I'm better at sorting out my feelings now, I'd like to talk about how we can make more space for me in our conversations," or "I relied on your steadiness for so long. Now that I've found my own inner steadiness, I'd like to explore other ways we can nurture each other."

One man revealed:

A terrifying change in his partner's health years ago brought up fears and uncertainties that he shared with his wife. His revealing brought them closer. He contrasted that with the fear and insecurity he felt when she later received a big promotion at work, noting how these vulnerabilities were much more difficult for him to reveal: "It struck me that I could share my fear of her dying, but not my fear of her getting a promotion because the promotion was really about my insecurity and worry that she wouldn't want me anymore. My fear of rejection was intense, but once I shared it and felt her response, it became manageable. Now I can honestly say to her, 'I'm so proud of you. I want you to shine as brightly as you can,' and we are closer than ever."

Another form of maintenance is the cultivation of gratitude for how and who you are to each other. In her article "Gratitude Is for Lovers," Amie Gordon found that in healthy relationships, gratitude creates cycles of generosity that enhance feelings of commitment and become self-sustaining. Gratitude is highly beneficial in transitions as well.

Parting Ways

Separation or divorce often creates pain and tumultuous feelings for all involved due to a range of disappointments, disagreements, and the dissolution of a relationship with someone who has been your primary person in life.

If interactions are still desired or necessary (e.g., while determining separation logistics, during coparenting, or because you'd like to continue to be in each other's lives in a new way), the first, second, and fourth Spotlight giving Moves are the same (i.e., "I'm so glad you told me," "Of course you feel _____," and "Is there anything else about this?").

The items on the menu of options for the third giving Move, "What do you need?" will likely change as the nature of the relationship changes. Rather than asking for physically intimate contact like affection, perhaps one or both partners will now benefit from more time problem-solving or from giving and receiving extra reassurance. Maybe they will add new menu items, such as "Remembering good moments from our time together," or "Creating a shared narrative so we can move into this next phase feeling more settled."

The receiving Moves ("I am able to receive" or "I am not able to receive") will stay the same and remain an important part of the process.

The revealing Moves are the ones that will likely change the most. Once partners are no longer primary for each other, then what, when, where, how, and how much they reveal of their inner worlds usually changes dramatically. Although this is an easy shift for some partners, many, even the ones who initially wanted or thought they wanted the divorce, experience tremendous grief.

Imagine how many times over the course of your relationship you have turned to your partner with your love or your distress. All these moments created habits in your thinking, feeling, and behavior. If, suddenly, this person isn't there in the same way, then what's asked of you is to develop new habits at every level of your being.

Is it any wonder many divorcing partners experience pain and conflict? Primary attachments run deep. Although the impact depends largely on the quality and perceived quality of the relationship prior to divorce (Vitelli 2015), breakups that include rejection by one or both partners register as pain in many of the same regions of the brain that become active when we break a bone (Weir 2012).

Changes in the way you interact with your former partner following divorce often take time and require tremendous individual support. The lingering cultural stigma of divorce can mean this healthy support is hard to find. Even when someone dies, survivors are often expected to be over it within a few months or a year. With divorce, no rituals exist for saying goodbye, and fewer casseroles are left on doorsteps.

If you have children together, advice for harmonious coparenting is easily found (i.e., "Communicate and keep the needs of the children first"). I could add, "Do your Spotlight Moves!" Sometimes divorcing couples can pick up some Moves that are helpful, although many who are in the thick of it understandably say something like, "Well, if we could *do that* [Spotlight Moves], then we probably wouldn't be divorcing."

When faced with conflict or confusion during marriage, partners often place their significant other in the role of the bad or wrong one (Atkinson 2006). This tendency is amplified during divorce as partners try to reckon with an outcome that is certainly not what they intended when they spoke their vows. *And,* when they share a vision, some former partners *do* find their way to being on the same side.

As one divorced person shared:

> We were each other's family, and we didn't want to lose that. We didn't want our kids to lose that. It's taken many years, but we are happy in our own lives and enjoy our new relationship as coparents. There's a lot of love and warmth when we're all together.

The Field

Whatever the stage of your relationship, whatever your current level of goodness of fit, when there's something you deeply want and you're willing, what might happen next?

> "Out beyond ideas of wrongdoing
> and rightdoing, there is a field.
> I'll meet you there."
>
> —RUMI

* * *

Summary

Long-term relationships weave a fabric that includes your people, places, practical lives, practices, memories, and more. With so much to potentially lose or recommit to, willingness takes on even greater proportions.

 In Which Direction Lies Your Growth?

- What hurts and losses might need to be grieved so something new can grow?
- For what are you grateful?
- How do you think about or approach forgiveness?
- Do you have unwanted images that take up space in your mind?
- What is your vision? Is there something you deeply want?

CONCLUSION

—

As partners, you will thrive where there's goodness of fit and the process of inviting, validating, reflecting, and supporting each other in a balanced way works so well that life events and your usual hot-button topics become opportunities for you to discover and continually rediscover: You've got this! You can reach for you partner while holding onto yourself. You can give generously, reveal vulnerably, and receive courageously for the benefit of yourself, your partner, and your relationship.

Along the way, whenever a pattern of conflict repeats, you learn that you likely have different ways of coping when you start to feel disconnected. Each of these coping styles impact the other person in ways you might not have guessed. What looks like not caring is often caring so much that you can do remarkably unhelpful things in the moment. Through the repetition and precision of the Spotlight, you have the opportunity to overcome the challenges of negative cycles and confusing content and implement new, helpful Moves that start you down the path of self-discovery, reconnection, and clarity.

We are indeed wired for connection, *and* we are better able to connect clearly when we have a secure handle on our own being. For any stage of relationship, the Spotlight serves to help us process losses, enhance gratitude, and reach for a shared narrative from which to move forward.

When we as people are activated to fear, we can quickly lose our usual abilities to solve problems together and instead fall into you-versus-me thinking, highlighting the ongoing dynamic tension that exists between independence and connection. *How do I hold onto me and reach for you?* is our perennial underlying question.

Throughout the book, I recommend various therapies and ideas for resolving blocks to giving, revealing, and receiving. Even when blocks to reconnection are removed, very often, partners aren't sure what to do or say next. Many of us simply are not taught such skills. Some people long for scripts, whereas for others can feel forced. Once you know the land, you will surely set aside the Mad Libs map. Until then, I invite you to bring it along to help you get started and to hold in your mind for the times you might feel lost.

Once you have a reliable, balanced, and loving way to work through the inevitable disconnections that arise from being in a relationship with another person, you can cocreate a foundation of loving care and attention, like the couple in the beginning of the book. Their argument wasn't about the dishes but about their responsiveness to each other. "There's so much that's good between us," they said. Now, rather than losing ground, they have a new ground of togetherness to walk upon.

HOW THE SPOTLIGHT
DEVELOPED

As a child, I believed if we could just talk about it, things would be okay. As an adult who is also a couples therapist, I understand sometimes we can't "Just talk about it," and often nobody feels okay until we can slow things down and get to the tender heart of what's really happening. Love as a feeling or love in action is nearly always present between partners, even if obscured. My search for this "talking about it" led to the development of the Spotlight and the writing of this book.

A Complement

Like many therapists, I rely on an eclectic blend of modalities. The two most prominent for me are the evidenced-based models of Eye Movement Desensitization and Reprocessing (EMDR) and Emotionally Focused Therapy (EFT). EMDR facilitates the processing of trauma and stressful events to bring an individual's inner stress cycles to completion so bodies, hearts, and minds can return to resting and expansive states. Emotionally Focused Therapy helps intimate partners strengthen and repair their emotional bonds by accessing the softer feelings hidden beneath their coping with disconnection.

Even with the brilliant guidance of these two models, my clients and I would reach points at which something more was needed to create reliable positive responsiveness between them. Although many partners had greatly reduced their reactivity and were feeling love for each other once again, they still needed consistently reliable steps they could remember outside of our sessions to help them break their old negative cycles.

The Moves also proved to be beneficial as an assessment, a way to see where trauma work or particular steps of EFT might best be focused.

Even when partners experience trauma reactions in their relationship, once they understand the Spotlight will come back to them in a reliable way, they often say something like, "Oh, I can do this [be in the Giving role of the Spotlight]." With a strong container for thoughts and feelings and a trust in the balance and flow of the relationship, people often discover their capacity for giving is greater than they realize. As van der Kolk stated, "Traumatized people fear ending up on the losing side once again." As partners alternate between Giving and Receiving roles, they find there is no losing side.

The Intention of Attention

David Russell, a mentor in my training on traumatic stress, first introduced me to William James's psychological model of the spotlight, which proposes that visual attention works similarly to that of a spotlight with a focal point in which things are viewed clearly. The area surrounding this focal point—known as the fringe—is still visible but not clearly seen. Dr. Russell taught this as a way to help direct a client's attention productively during trauma therapy: to use their attention as a spotlight rather than a window.

In EFT, the therapist gives clear direction of attention to one partner and then to the other, and then for partners speaking directly to each other. Just like artists, dancers, musicians, athletes, improvisers, and anyone focused on their endeavor, therapists are continually choosing what to pay attention to in a session and what to set aside for later. Clients benefit when choosing with conscious intention as well.

As William James said, "The art of being wise is the art of knowing what to overlook," and, with that, the corollary of knowing what to look upon.

Hurt and confusion arise for couples who aren't clearly seen—and aren't clearly seeing.

Very often, what couples want is all possible, just not all at once. When there is conflict, we have to slow things down, and the movement of the spotlight visual gives us something memorable to relate to when our brains get all righteous or jumbly because we want to rely on our person and disconnection from them is likely scary to us on some level.

The phrases of the Moves were chosen as my clients and I gravitated toward language that was effective and simple enough to be remembered in a stressful moment. Even the most magnificent ideas aren't helpful if you can't remember them when you need them. For this reason, we use sentence starters so you don't have to translate the concepts. The beginning dialogue is right there to start you down the path.

It's Not Genuine If You Tell Me What to Say

I understand this concern. I value authenticity, too, *and* you're asking so much of yourself to go free-form in moments when you might also be working to calm yourself down inside. It would be like performing on the biggest stage without any structure to guide you or contain your energy.

Origins of The Moves That Make the Model

Giving Move 1: "I'm so glad you told me."

For many, revealing something that brings up difficult feelings and then hearing someone you love say, "I'm so glad you told me," brings relief.

As I was learning to become the mom I wanted to be, I would ask my first therapist, the late Dr. Marguerite Pengel, for guidance about how to handle my own feelings when my young children were angry or sad (feelings were overwhelming for me back then). She gave me this gem that is now the first Move of the Spotlight Giving role. She told me to say to them, "I'm so glad you told me." This one made my brain hurt for a while until I got it. Some part of me *was* entirely grateful they were telling me, even though other parts of me weren't so sure. The phrase not only soothed them, it also shifted me into the mindset I wanted to be in when they came to me with their feelings.

Giving Move 2: "Of course you feel _____."

Validating someone's feelings and then reflecting the meaning they are making are the powerhouses of skill for knowing a person and helping them feel known. I'm grateful to have been exposed to these skills by teachers, authors, friends, and colleagues, and intensively during EFT trainings.

Giving Move 3: "Do you know what you need?" and Move 4: "Is there anything else about this?"

These two Moves crystallized with a group of colleagues when we would practice our validating and reflecting skills. As our friendships grew beyond the classes, we noticed we didn't always want validation or reflection when we shared something difficult from our own lives, so we started asking,

"What do you need?" In a sense, we were creating a menu of flexible options.

Giving Move 4: "Is there anything else about this?" bookends the giving Moves with the energy of invitation.

Receiving and Revealing Moves

Revealing authentically from vulnerability is the aim of many approaches. The additional step of having partners pause to notice and share their level of receiving has become key to cocreating partnership and identifying where interactions break down and need attention.

Illustrations

From my earliest dreams of this project, images of characters appeared alongside. I suspected we (reader and author) would welcome some opportunities to laugh at ourselves and our funny beingness while exploring these serious and important topics. I shared my imagined scenes with artist Michael Scott, and our collaboration for the book and videos began.

(Preliminary sketches.)

ACKNOWLEDGMENTS

———

With gratitude:

To Eric Koester, Regina Stribling, Kaity Van Riper, Zvonimir Bulaja, and the teams at Book Creators and New Degree Press. For your teaching, editing, design, and support throughout this writing and publishing journey. Kaity, for your guidance and attuned responsiveness. Regina, for helping me hold what felt like an infinite number of pieces until they began to take form, and Eric, for your vision, enthusiasm, and the remarkable opportunities you create. Thank you

For a group of women at Speaker Sisterhood. Several of these chapters were seeded in the talks I shared with you. Your encouragement mattered.

For the late Francine Shapiro, founder of EMDR, and Deany Laliotis, the teacher who helped me learn to interweave for interdependence. For Sue Johnson, founder of EFT, and for the vibrant EFT community. For James Osborne, who convinced me trading *but* for *and* was a good deal. For David

Russell, a gifted researcher and therapist in the healing of trauma. Thank you for your teachings. For my clients, who are my teachers every day.

For Nora Jamieson and Laurie Roberts, who taught me that grief is life-giving.

For the many friends who encouraged and supported me, read for me, and offered their wisdom to this work. Listed in the order we appeared in each other's lives: Lisa Goolsby, Annette Herron, Rebecca Kronk, Beth Ann Calhoun, Julia Lawrence, Denise Eckman, Jackie Hudnell, Jamie Miller, Kristina Biondolillo, Lissa Perez, Brice Hall, Jackie Crowley, Tom Crowley, Karen Smyth, Ellen Bowdon, Wendy Madigan, Kelly Conway, Deirdre Lloyd, Beth Schave-Bemis, Pam Briggs, Dave Briggs, Lorri Fitzsimmons, Kristin Flyntz, Joanna Karp, Macdara MacColl, Stephen Diana, Jim Young, Paul Bailin, Sally Ekus, and Zoann Guernsey, my heartfelt thanks.

For Cruger Johnson Phillips, Christopher Roberts, Pam Victor, and Laurie Roberts. Thank you for your time, expert interviews, and belief in me.

For Michael Scott, who brought what I could see in my mind to the page in the form of two stretchy characters. Thank you for your artistic talent, your flexibility, and your willingness. I greatly value our collaboration.

For my family. Thank you all for loving and supporting me— especially Lisa, Mark, Kristina, and Papa, for your influence and involvement with this endeavor. For Unc, who gave me the gift of time, and for Robertjohn, who read with enthusiastic feedback and a keen eye.

Special love for my furry four-leggeds, who clearly pursue and withdraw according to the topics *they* care about.

For the memory of my mother, Jacque Herron. How I loved writing with you at the kitchen table. Your joy and our playfulness with words live in me.

For the memory of my father, Paul Brady, the most voracious reader of the most esoteric tomes. I miss you.

For Joanna Karp and Macdara MacColl. Our friendship delights, inspires, and teaches me again and again about the power of secure connection and Family. Mac, your accurate empathy and grasp of theory deeply inform and expand me. Jojo, for your wisdom and expertise, the countless hours, and your gentle, "Okay, let's struggle with this," whenever I felt stuck, my deepest gratitude.

For Tyler, Cameron, and Grant—the three extra hearts I have running around outside my body. Before you could walk or talk, you taught me how to see. Thank you for your reading, encouragement, and love.

For Jim—my friend, my love, and my partner. Your willingness to explore life and a relationship with me is both exhilarating and deeply soothing. "We got this!"

For those who contributed your wisdom and stories—you make this book real.

REFERENCES

___

Introduction

Hanh, Thich Nhat. *How to Love.* Berkeley: Parallax Press, 2014.

Johnson, Sue. *Hold Me Tight: Seven Conversations for a Lifetime of Love.* New York: Little, Brown Spark, 2008.

O'Donohue, John. *Beauty: The Invisible Embrace. Rediscovering the True Sources of Compassion, Serenity, and Hope.* Read by John O'Donohue. Louisville: Sounds True, 2015. Audible audio ed., 5 hr. 18 min.

Van der Kolk, Bessel. *The Body Keeps the Score: Brain, Mind, and Body in the Healing of Trauma.* New York: Penguin, 2014.

Chapter 1

Gordon, Gwen. "Well Played: The Origins and Future of Playfulness." *American Journal of Play* 6, no. 2 (Winter 2014): 234-266. https://files.eric.ed.gov/fulltext/EJ1023802.pdf.

Gottman, John, and Julie Schwartz Gottman. *The Science of Couples and Family Therapy: Behind the Scenes at the Love Lab.* New York: W. W. Norton & Company, 2018.

Martin, Matthew, and Eric C. Cowan. "Remembering Martin Buber and the I—Thou in Counseling." *Counseling Today* (member insights), American Counseling Association. May 8, 2019. https://ct.counseling.org/2019/05/remembering-martin-buber-and-the-i-thou-in-counseling/.

New Degree Press—Our Authors. "Cheli Lange, LPC Spotlight of Love." Mar 29, 2022. 2:15. https://youtu.be/nHExcQxG4Dg.

Newberg, Andrew, and Mark Robert Waldman. *Words Can Change Your Brain: 12 Conversation Strategies to Build Trust, Resolve Conflict, and Increase Intimacy*. New York: Avery, 2013.

Chapter 2

Brach, Tara. *Radical Acceptance: Embracing Your Life with the Heart of a Buddha*. New York: Random House Publishing Group, 2004.

Jason Headley. "It's Not About the Nail." May 22, 2013. 1:41. https://youtu.be/-4EDhdAHrOg.

Chapter 3

Kelly, Jane. "We Asked an Expert Why We Hold Hands, and Learned It's Good for You." *UVA Today*. February 13, 2020. https://news.virginia.edu/content/we-asked-expert-why-we-hold-hands-and-learned-its-good-you.

Siegel, Daniel. *The Mindful Therapist: A Clinician's Guide to Mindsight and Neural Integration*. New York: W. W. Norton & Company, 2010.

Chapter 4

Van der Kolk, Bessel. "Trauma in the Body: An Interview with Dr. Bessel van der Kolk." By Elissa Melaragno. *Daily Good.* April 21, 2018. https://www.dailygood.org/story/1901/trauma-in-the-body-an-interview-with-dr-bessel-van-der-kolk-elissa-melaragno/.

Chapter 5

Gable, Shelly L., Gian C. Gonzaga, and Amy Strachman. "Will you be there for me when things go right? Supportive responses to positive event disclosures." *Journal of Personality and Social Psychology* 91, no. 5 (2006): 904-917. https://doi.org/10.1037/0022-3514.91.5.904.

Hendrix, Harville, and Helen LaKelley Hunt. *Getting the Love You Want: A Guide for Couples: Third Edition.* New York: St. Martin's Griffin, 2019.

Levine, Peter A. *In an Unspoken Voice: How the Body Releases Trauma and Restores Goodness.* Berkeley: North Atlantic Books, 2010.

Rosenberg, Marshall B. *Nonviolent Communication: A Language of Life: Life-Changing Tools for Healthy Relationships (Nonviolent Communication Guides).* Encinitas: PuddleDancer Press, 2015.

Weiss, Paul, Brent Atkinson, Ahna Holzinger-Young, and Anna Larsen., "An Application of Pragmatic/Experiential Therapy for Couples." In *Case Studies in Couples Therapy: Theory based approaches,* edited by D. K. Carson & M. Casado-Kehoe, 249-261. Routledge/Taylor & Francis Group, 2011. Kindle.

Chapter 6

Golden, Bernard. "How Disavowed Anger Contributes to Suffering: Anger that is denied doesn't go away. It demands our attention." *Psychology Today,* April 6, 2019. https://www.psychologytoday. com/us/blog/overcoming-destructive-anger/201904/how-disavowed-anger-contributes-suffering.

Gottman, John Mordechai. *Marital Interaction: Experimental Investigations.* Cambridge: Academic Press, 1979.

Nepo, Mark. *The Book of Awakening: Having the Life You Want by Being Present to the Life You Have.* Newburyport: Red Wheel, 2020.

Chapter 7

Berne, Eric. *Games People Play: The Basic Handbook of Transactional Analysis.* New York: Ballantine Books, 1996.

Weinhold, Barry and Janae B. Weinhold. *How to Break Free of the Drama Triangle and Victim Consciousness.* Scotts Valley: CreateSpace Independent Publishing Platform, 2014.

Chapter 8

Bretherton, Inge. "The Origins of Attachment Theory: John Bowlby and Mary Ainsworth." *Developmental Psychology* 28, no. 5 (1992): 759-775. https://cmapspublic2.ihmc.us/rid=1LQX400NM-RBVKH9-1KL6/the%20origins%20of%20attachment%20 theory%20john%20bowlby%20and_mary_ainsworth.pdf.

Katz, L. F. and J. M. Gottman. "Patterns of Marital Conflict Predict Children's Internalizing and Externalizing Behaviors," *Developmental Psychology* 29, no. 6 (1993): 940-950.

Levine, Amir, and Rachel Heller. *Attached: The New Science of Adult Attachment and How It Can Help You Find—and Keep—Love.* New York: Bluebird Publishing, 2019. Kindle.

Mikulincer, Mario, and Phillip R. Shaver. *Attachment in Adulthood, Second Edition: Structure, Dynamics, and Change.* New York: Guilford Press, 2016.

Schrodt, Paul, Paul L. Witt, and Jenna Shimkowski, "A Meta-Analytical Review of the Demand/Withdraw Pattern of Interaction and Its Associations with Individual, Relational, and Communicative Outcomes." *Communication Monographs* 81, no. 1 (January 2014): 28-58.

Chapter 9

Perry, B. D., Pollard, R. A., Blakley, T. L., Baker, W. L. and Vigilante, D. "Childhood trauma, the neurobiology of adaptation, and 'use-dependent' development of the brain: How 'states' become traits.'" *Infant Mental Health Journal* 16 (1995): 271-291.

Chapter 10

Gallant, Paul and Ilene Strauss. "Narrative Therapy with Couples." In *Case Studies in Couples Therapy: Theory based approaches*, edited by D. K. Carson & M. Casado-Kehoe, Routledge/Taylor & Francis Group, 2011. Kindle.

Johnson, Sue. *Love Sense: The Revolutionary New Science of Romantic Relationships.* New York: Little Brown Spark, 2013., Kindle.

Linder, Jason N., Alba Niño, Sesen Negash, and Sandra Espinoza. "Thematic Analysis of Therapists' Experiences Integrating EMDR and EFT in Couple Therapy: Theoretical and Clinical Complementarity, and Benefits to Client Couples." *Journal of Marital and Family Therapy* (2022): 1-21. https://doi.org/10.1111/jmft.12587.

Chapter 11

Bowen, Murray. *Family Therapy in Clinical Practice*. Lanham: Jason Aronson, Inc., 1993.

Chaplin, Tara M. "Gender and Emotion Expression: A Developmental Contextual Perspective." *Emotion Review* 7, no. 1 (2015): 14-21. doi:10.1177/1754073914544408.

Klemp, Nate, and Kaley Klemp. *The 80/80 Marriage: A New Model for a Happier, Stronger Relationship*. London: Penguin Life, 2021.

Page, Ken. *Deeper Dating: How to Drop the Games of Seduction and Discover the Power of Intimacy*. Boulder: Shambhala, 2014.

Prior, M. D. Smart, A Sanson, and F. Oberklaid. "Sex Differences in Psychological Adjustment from Infancy to 8 Years." *Journal of American Academy of Child & Adolescent Psychiatry* 32, no. 2 (1993): 291-304. https://pubmed.ncbi.nlm.nih.gov/8444757/.

Vaughan, Diane. *Uncoupling: Turning Points in Intimate Relationships*. New York: Vintage, 1990.

Weigard, Alexander., Amy M. Loviska, and Adriene M. Beltz. "Little Evidence for Sex or Ovarian Hormone Influences on Affective Variability." *Scientific Reports* 11, (2021): 20925. https://doi.org/10.1038/s41598-021-00143-7.

Chapter 12

Albom, Mitch. *Tuesday with Morrie*. New York: Doubleday, 1997.

Banker, Jamie E., Christine E. Kaestle, and Katherine Allen. "Dating Is Hard Work: A Narrative Approach to Understanding Sexual and Romantic Relationships in Young Adulthood." *Contemporary Family Therapy* 32 (2010): 173-191. https://doi.org/10.1007/s10591-009-9111-9.

Fritz, Robert. *Creating: A practical guide to the creative process and how to use it to create anything—a work of art, a relationship, a career or a better life*. New York: Ballantine Books, 1993.

Markus, Hazel, and Paula Nurius. "Possible Selves." *American Psychologist* 41, no. 9 (1986): 954-969. https://doi.org/10.1037/0003-066X.41.9.954.

Zentman, Michael D., "Integrated Couple Therapy: A Family Developmental Approach to the Treatment of Couples Incorporating Psychoanalytic and Systemic Models." In *Case Studies in Couples Therapy (Routledge Series on Family Therapy and Counseling)*, edited by David K. Carson and Montserrat Casado-Kehoe. New York: Taylor and Francis, 2013. Kindle Edition.

Chapter 13

Aponte, Catherine. "The Right Way to Negotiate with Your Partner." *Psychology Today*, February 15, 2019. https://www.psychologytoday.com/us/blog/marriage-equals/201902/the-right-way-negotiate-your-partner.

Fry, Hannah. "The Mathematics of Love." Filmed February 2015 at Binghamton University: NY. TED video, 16:53. https://www.ted.com/talks/hannah_fry_the_mathematics_of_love.

Jay, Meg. *The Defining Decade: Why Your Twenties Matter—and How to Make the Most of Them Now.* New York: Twelve, 2021.

Levine, Amir, and Rachel Heller. *Attached: The New Science of Adult Attachment and How It Can Help You Find—and Keep—Love.* New York: Bluebird Publishing, 2019. Kindle.

Olson-Sigg, Amy, and David. H. Olson. "PREPARE/ENRICH Program for Premarital and Married Couples." *In Case Studies in Couples Therapy,* edited by David K. Carson and M. Casado-Kehoe, 1-12. New York: Routledge Publisher, 2011. https://132h243xsp5946a1f2c18k9z-wpengine.netdna-ssl.com/wp-content/uploads/2020/12/pe_customized_case_study.pdf.

Palmer, Parker. "The Broken-Open Heart: Living with Faith and Hope in the Tragic Gap." *Weavings: A Journal of the Christian Spiritual Life* 24: no. 2 (March/April 2009). https://couragerenewal.org/wp-content/uploads/2022/06/PJP-WeavingsArticle-Broken-OpenHeart.pdf.

Powell, Alvin. "When Love and Science Double Date." *The Harvard Gazette.* February 13, 2018. https://news.harvard.edu/gazette/story/2018/02/scientists-find-a-few-surprises-in-their-study-of-love/.

Ryan, K. D., J. M. Gottman, J. D. Murray, S. Carrere, and C. Swanson (2000). Theoretical and Mathematical Modeling of Marriage. In M. Lewis and I. Granic (eds.), *Emotion, Development, and Self-Organization: Dynamic Systems Approaches to Emotional Development,* Cambridge University Press.

Wu, Katherine. "Love, Actually: The Science Behind Lust, Attraction, and Companionship." *Harvard University: The Graduate School of Arts and Sciences* (blog), February 14, 2017. https://sitn.hms.harvard.edu/flash/2017/love-actually-science-behind-lust-attraction-companionship/.

Chapter 14

Atkinson, Brent J. "Rewiring Emotional Habits: The Pragmatic/ Experiential Method." In *Clinical Casebook of Couple Therapy*, edited by A. S. Gurman, 181-207. New York: Guilford Press, 2010.

Cain, Susan. *Bittersweet: How Sorrow and Longing Make Us Whole.* New York: Crown, 2022.

Gordon, Amie M. "Gratitude Is for Lovers." *Greater Good Magazine.* February 5, 2013.

Johnson, Susan M., Judy A. Makinen, and John W. Millikin. "Attachment Injuries in Couple Relationships: A New Perspective on Impasses in Couples Therapy." *Journal of Marital and Family Therapy* 27, no. 2 (April 2001): 145-55. doi:10.1111/j.1752-0606.2001.tb01152.x. PMID: 11314548.

Kysely, Andrea, Brian Bishop, Robert Kane, Maryanne Cheng, Mia De Palma, and Rosanna Rooney. "Expectations and Experiences of Couples Receiving Therapy Through Videoconferencing: A Qualitative Study." *Frontiers in Psychology* 10, (2020): 2992. https://doi.org/10.3389%2Ffpsyg.2019.02992.

Rumi, Jalal al-Din. *The Essential Rumi, New Expanded Edition.* Translation by Coleman Barks. San Francisco: HarperOne, 2004.

Shapiro, Francine, Florence W. Kaslow, and Louise Maxfield, eds. *Handbook of EMDR and Family Therapy Processes*, Hoboken: Wiley, 2007.

Vitelli, Romeo. "Life After Divorce: Is divorce always going to have a negative impact on the people involved?" *Psychology Today.* July 13, 2015. https://www.psychologytoday.com/us/blog/media-spotlight/201507/life-after-divorce.

Weir, Kirsten. "The Pain of Social Rejection: As Far as the Brain is Concerned, a Broken Heart May Not Be So Different from a Broken Arm." *Monitor on Psychology* 43, no. 4 (2020): 50. https://www.apa.org/monitor/2012/04/rejection.

Made in the USA
Monee, IL
17 October 2022

16058446R00144